The Successful Golfer
Practical Fixes for the Mental Game of Golf

Dr. Paul McCarthy and Dr. Marc Jones

BENNION KEARNY

Published in 2013 by Bennion Kearny Limited.

ISBN: 978-1-909125-23-0

Published by Bennion Kearny Limited
6 Victory House
64 Trafalgar Road
Birmingham
B13 8BU

www.BennionKearny.com

Cover image: © Shutterstock/ssuaphotos

For Lesley, Liam and Euan

- Paul -

For Helen, Molly, Jacob and all my family

- Marc -

About The Authors

Dr Paul McCarthy is a Lecturer in Psychology at Glasgow Caledonian University. He has published numerous academic papers and books in sport and exercise psychology. He is a registered Sport Psychologist (HCPC) with over 15 years of experience working as a consultant in amateur and professional golf.

Dr Marc Jones is a Reader in Sport and Exercise Psychology at Staffordshire University and has published over forty academic papers mostly in the area of stress and emotion. He is a registered Sport Psychologist (HCPC) and is currently working as a consultant in professional football and golf.

Acknowledgements

We are most grateful to Bennion Kearny for the opportunity to publish with them. We are especially thankful to James Lumsden-Cook for his helpful suggestions, practical advice, and guidance whilst preparing and publishing this book. Finally, we are indebted to every amateur and professional golfer who sought our help to become a successful golfer.

Table of Contents

difference

for the best outcomes in golf?

The Successful Golfer

Part 1

Introduction

The width of any green, the length of any putt, or the height of any putter, is just 5 1/2 inches - the space between your ears

Bobby Jones

If you play golf, you might think that much of this book is common sense. Though it might be common sense, it is often not common practice. In other words, most readers will be aware that they need to work on "the space between their ears" to succeed in golf but they do not always practise what is best for them. For instance, most golfers know that their short game is the key to lowering their scores yet it is common to see driving ranges full and short-game practice areas empty.

The enjoyment most golfers receive from practising and excelling at the long game is much stronger than the enjoyment they receive from practising and excelling at the short game. Seeing the ball fly on a perfect trajectory to a tight pin on a small green is what gains most applause around the golf course and a feeling of success for the golfer. Rolling in the putt for a birdie doesn't seem to offer that same feeling. Yet, it is the part that matters most.

Successful golfers are people who know that much of what is written here is common sense but they are making this common sense their common practice. They have learned to get more enjoyment from the short game than from the long game. They know that the long game is important but they love practising the short game even more. They know that the "space between their ears" is vital to success so they integrate it into their practice and competitive golf. The successful golfer will gain most from this book because the successful golfer is always looking for ways to improve.

The Successful Golfer

Our advice is simple. First, make a commitment to practise smarter (you'll learn how to practise smarter in this book) and maximise your return from the short game.

Second, spend time planning your tee shots and preparing psychologically before you play each round of golf.

Third, be proud of the process (i.e., your pre-shot routine) you have developed to hit each shot on the golf course, and learn to accept the outcome of each shot - whatever happens.

Finally, accept yourself as a good person who plays golf well rather than a good person *because* you play golf well.

If you do these things, we are sure that golf will be a success in your life and you'll be able to say what Byron Nelson proclaimed many years after he put away his clubs: "I am exactly happy. I got what I wanted from golf. I've had a good, warm, inward feeling all my life."

The Differences Among Golfers

Over the years, we have learned that some golfers do not improve for one reason or another, but often because of a poor mental game. These golfers live on technical answers to all of golf's problems but these explanations fall short when the greatest golfers in the game remind us how 'what they think' is so important. Arnold Palmer said: "You play from the shoulders up. It isn't all-important, just 90% and maybe over 90%."

The greatest golfers relish competition; they don't hide from it. Seve Ballesteros explained that: "Golf has always been my passion and competing has always been great. It's one thing I always like and enjoy - I like to feel the pressure."

It seems fair to state that the greatest achievements in golf are built between the ears. The happiness quote, above, comes from Byron Nelson – a man who won 11 tournaments in a row in 1945. He said: "What I did in 1945 was a mental achievement. In those days I could drive the ball so well I would really get bored. I just decided I was not going to hit one careless shot. Plus, I had the focus of the ranch [Nelson needed $55,000 to buy the ranch in Texas where he would live for the next 60 years]. I was almost in a trance. I guess what they call it now is being in a zone. Any time you have a record that stands for 60 years, you've done something pretty good."

In this chapter, we shall introduce you to two ways of thinking, feeling, and behaving. You might identify with one way or both ways at different times. We refer to them as the *Old Course* and the *New Course*; the golfers who play at the Old Course think differently, feel differently, and behave differently to those who play at the New Course.

The Old Course

Golfers at the Old Course love to play golf, seizing every chance to get onto the course or the range to hit a bucket of balls. They watch golf on TV, read golf magazines and buy golf equipment to improve their game. If they get an opportunity, they attend a major event or the Ryder Cup. These golfers are like most golfers because they want to play golf, enjoy it, and play better, especially if they play golf competitively.

On the Range at The Old Course

When golfers from the Old Course get a chance to practise, they head down to the practice range. They head straight to the counter for a bucket of balls or maybe two buckets if they have time.

Buckets and clubs in hand, they search for a free driving bay, especially one with a good mat or maybe one with a mirror to keep a check on mechanics if things start to go wrong. They like to occupy their usual bay because that is what they are used to, and they don't like anyone upsetting their routine because it disrupts them.

When they get in to the bay, they put their bucket of balls down and get right to it. They might think to themselves, "Well I probably should warm up with a driver because if I don't drive well, my game will fall apart." So they tee up the ball and boom – a duck hook. "Damn! What happened there? I think I know. It must have been my hands turning over at impact." Then they tell themselves, "Right, extend through the shot, that's what I need to do."

They tee up the second ball, and boom, a second duck hook. Okay! Try again and so on until yes – a soaring drive, straight as a die, down the range easily past the 250-yard marker. They hold rigid expectations of how they should perform – "I must not hit poor shots."

Next, these golfers say, "Right, I will give that club a rest and get to work on my long-irons because, last Sunday, they couldn't have been any worse – I was embarrassed on the 18th fairway with that shot to the green. It landed in the bunker and I made a six on the par five. If my long-irons were better I would have walked off with a birdie at least. So here goes." After ten attempts, one long iron resembles the trajectory of a professional's shot. "Yes, that is what I have been looking for!" Overall, the nine previous shots didn't seem to have any routine to them; just put a ball down on the mat and hit it. No proper set-up, just get the ball out there as fast as possible because, after all, there are lots of balls to get through.

And this regime continues day after day, every time golfers from the Old Course head down to the range. They journey to the range because the golf magazines have convinced them that their faults can be fixed if they just change one part of their set-up or ball position. But each month, the advice changes somewhat and in the end it is very confusing.

After months of anguish on the range, and on the course, it seems the only solution is to see the professional for an assessment. "If my swing was sorted out I wouldn't have many problems, no problems maybe, in my game – I would definitely improve my handicap!"

Golfers at the Old Course have purchased lots of equipment, the best of everything to make the game a success, to conquer their handicap. They have an exotic range of training aids, for each segment of the swing, take away, backswing, downswing and follow through. Everything is mechanically driven and when all the parts are put together, then their swing will be perfect. Because they admire Ernie Els, they obsess about his swing. Or it could be Luke Donald or Tiger Woods or Padraig Harrington. The main point is that their own swing, the one that is natural and owned by them, is not perceived to be good enough. It is not a swing that is worthy of being seen on the first tee of the golf course. It is not a swing that shows their confidence because they lack confidence in their own ability.

These golfers have forgotten what has helped the professionals gain the swings they have, the countless hours of practice, but also the trust in their own capacity and ability to judge their swing as useful and appropriate for them.

When the golfers at the Old Course go see a golf tournament and watch the professionals in the practice area, they should recognise that each swing is unique. It would be impossible to find two swings that are exactly the same in every way. All golfers are trying to do the same thing, to keep the clubface square at impact - but how they get there is different. Remember, these professional golfers have honed their skills to represent them at major golf tournaments and they trust their swing. Yes, they want to improve and, yes, they change aspects of their swing but most importantly they are doing what is natural and owned by them. They are proud of their swing technique because it is theirs – they *want* to own their swing.

The golfers at the Old Course cannot get away from the long game; they believe that mastering their long game will advance their golf game most. The other aspects of pitching, chipping, bunker shots and putting can take care of themselves. Anyway, what fun is there in rolling a putt on the putting green when I can boom a 300-yard drive down the fairway? And to practise bunker shots means getting sand in my shoes and on my clubs and I have just washed them to come down to the range. I can do some pitching here on the range mat if I have to, just a few shots to these markers because that is exactly how the game will be. And chipping, well there is not much to that game really. I do my chipping when I warm up for a game on Sunday if I have time. So my short game is fine, it's just the long game that needs sorting out.

These are the beliefs of an Old Course golfer, and they know them to be true. The only road to success lies in mastering the swing. Now, let us meet the golfers on The New Course. Something about them seems different.

The New Course

We have seen how Golfers at the Old Course love to play golf. They grab every chance to get onto the course or go down the range. Golf on television and in magazines is always present, and new golf equipment is always on order. If they get an opportunity, they attend a major. These golfers are like most golfers because they want to play golf, take pleasure in it, and play better. Do you feel like you might have read this somewhere before? Golfers on the New Course are like golfers on the Old Course, in many ways, but *how* they use their mind seems to make all the difference to how they practise and subsequently play.

On the Range at the New Course

When golfers from the New Course get a chance to practice, they head down to the range. They head straight for the counter for a bucket of balls or maybe two if they have the time. Buckets and balls in hand, they walk past all the driving bays and head for the short game area. They like the range and will return, to finish off the session, but they are wise about their game. They know only too well that the short game is the game that really matters. They are well aware that putting alone can make up forty percent of their strokes in a round of golf.

Like the players at the Old Course, they love the driving range with all the clean balls and perfect lies and plenty of targets to aim at - but they know that they need to attend to the short game.

Now, when the players at the New Course get to the short game area, they don't just put the bucket of balls down to start chipping or pitching. They begin with a plan. They know that they will spend their time chipping, pitching, putting, and in the sand, but how much time should they give to each part of the game? Well, that depends on how their game is going and what they have identified as the most important parts of their game to work on.

Next, they stretch to make sure they have a good range of movement in their wrists, shoulders, arms, and hips. They are ready to begin.

These golfers might have identified three skills to work on: 50-yard pitches, chipping from the light rough around the green, and 15-yard bunker shots. They have identified that they have an hour and a half to practice so they allocate 15 minutes to each of these parts of the short game, leaving 45 minutes for putting and the long game.

Because they only want to work on lag putting, they set aside 15 minutes for a specific drill to improve lag putting. The long game needs some attention, especially maintaining tempo, regardless of the club in their hands. The strategy is to work on sustaining a calm and relaxed pace to strike each ball. Then, they will finish with a putting drill. On another day, they might spend more time putting, stroking short putts to increase their confidence and feel for putting - completely trusting in each stroke they make.

These golfers begin with variable practice on the short game. This means that they hit a bunker shot and follow that shot with a chip from off the green. They might follow that shot with a pitch shot to a marker on the range. The discipline for such practice means that they can organise and prepare for each shot and execute each shot according to their routine.

Each shot requires them to be patient, assess the lie, and prepare mentally to execute the shot. One of the most important parts of practice is developing a routine that can *actually be used* on the golf course. Sometimes it is useful to spend time focusing on just one aspect of a skill and that requires a block of concentrated practice. Golfers at the New Course spend time going through the process of what they would do in a game situation. But the most important focus of their practice is that they are meticulous about their set-up and mental approach to each shot – that never changes, ever. Before each shot, they form a clear picture in their minds of what they would like to achieve before they attempt the shot.

If they are having a difficult practice session, and the outcome of each shot is not what they would like it to be, they do not get upset or start to blame someone (or something else) for their performance. They accept the outcome of each shot and prepare to execute the next shot with the same mental discipline as always. This is not easy but that is what makes them successful and happy golfers.

Each practice session has specific targets. Because golf is a target game, it makes sense to spend time working on hitting each shot to a target because it simulates what the game is going to present. These golfers can take their game to the course because they practise in a way that is so similar to the game on the course. They are wise – they remember to practise as they intend to play. They maintain composure by treating practice like competition and competition like practice.

To show you how they set goals for each drill or skill, these golfers might set aside six balls. With each shot, they trust themselves more and more and their eyes and thoughts are out into their target. They are going through their routine but each shot gives them a chance to trust themselves, and their swing, more and more. They become loose and relaxed. More loose and relaxed because they are only thinking about trusting their body to react athletically to each shot. That is the key to their success.

When New Course golfers head to the putting area, they are heading there with a plan. They constantly check and record their progress but they don't get caught up in evaluating themselves as golfers with each set of scores. They realise that there is variability to performance and they are willing to accept this variability.

They learn to leave their critical minds at the gate of the driving range or golf course. Critical minds have a time and function but not while they are focusing on playing their best. They want to do their best in a focused and relaxed way. A keen and unperturbed focus is what they are looking for – a focus that will last, and make the game the enjoyable experience that it should be. That is the great challenge for the golfers at the New Course.

On the putting green, New Course golfers are calm and relaxed because they enjoy putting. They love the short game and adore putting. They see putting as the key to excellence and enjoyment in golf. Putting is the way forward to lower their score but, at the same time, they don't *obsess* about the game of putting. It is a game within a game and they are happy to play that game. But what these golfers love about the game of putting is how they get a chance to roll the ball to the cup; they aim to putt their best each time the putter is in their hands. There is no time to be tentative – a free flowing athletic stroke is all that is on their minds.

To build some confidence they might work on two-foot putts – just listening to the putt hit the cup and enjoying the acoustic euphoria. Next, they might begin lag putting, but not to the cup. They want to work on feeling the distance. So they might putt to the fringe of the green and maintain the same keen focus on their game.

As you can see, the golfers from the New Course are only different in the way they play and enjoy the game because they think differently about the game. They have learned to coach their mind and their emotions to work for them rather than against them – that is their secret!

The golfers at the New Course play competitions with golfers at the Old Course. They don't always win but most of the time they win and they enjoy the game more. Because they enjoy the game more, they spend more time practising and their clear, focused practice brings the results that they seek. The handicaps tumble and their enjoyment rises. What more could any golfer ask from golf?

You know whether you are a golfer at the Old Course or at the New Course. There might be part of you in each course and you want to step to the New Course more fully and live its philosophy. Remember, the choice is yours.

How Should You Use This Book?

You might read this book through from cover to cover and put it away afterwards but this book should forever remain in your golf bag, or by your bedside, because it will help you to become a successful golfer.

This book is split into three sections so you can use it for your specific needs. In the first section we outline the 50 most common faults and practical fixes for the mental game of golf. In the second section we outline key research on the psychology of golf and suggest a practical technique based on the research to help you become a more successful golfer. Finally, in the third section we outline practical techniques for becoming a confident golfer. So whether you wish to fix a fault, read how the latest research can help you, or work on being a confident golfer - this book has a section for you. We believe this book will serve you best when you first check out how your golf game is going and see where you need to improve. Then pick one or two areas to work on at a time so you don't overload yourself and perform poorly. Do not try to fix everything at once. Remember, your game has developed over years of practice so you should allow your mental game to develop similarly. The good thing is that your mental game may already be quite advanced and just needs some pointers to help you get the most out of yourself. We wish you well on your journey to becoming a successful golfer.

At the start of each fault, we have also included a key to illustrate how common the fault is (5 golf balls is really common, 1 golf ball is rare), and how difficult it is to overcome (1 flag is easy, 5 flags means really difficult). Remember, these are the most common faults we have been presented with, by the amateur and professional golfers we have supported over the past 15 years. Golfers have rectified these faults by persevering with the suggested strategy to fix the fault. A sensible strategy and lots of effort will get you where you want to go.

How Common      How Difficult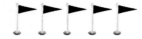
is the Fault   to Fix

Now, let's head to the course, and address one of the most common faults!

Fault 1: I never seem to be able to play as well on the course as I do on the range

How Common is the Fault    How Difficult to Fix

> " *Golf is one of the toughest sports mentally because it is the only sport where your opponent has no influence on the ball. You have to hold your own alone on a green. That kind of pressure means that the top golfers have a unique quality.* "
>
> **Peter Alliss** (golf commentator)

Many golfers are rarely able to replicate the way they play on the range with the way they play on the course. On the range they can drive the ball unerringly, chip and putt with ease. They expect a neat transition to the golf course.

It feels like there should be a logical link between practice and competition but it often baffles golfers to understand why the transfer from the range to the course is bumpy.

One of the reasons why some golfers do not play as well on the course as they do on the range is because the playing conditions differ measurably. A firm, flat mat does not give you a feel for the fairway or rough. It does not give you a demanding uphill or downhill lie, though some driving ranges do have such mechanical mats to replicate these conditions. Many driving ranges are undercover so the wind and rain do not interfere as much as they do when you are on the course. These changes in the environment offer remarkable challenges.

Many golfers seek the help of a golf coach or sport psychologist when they cannot explain their inconsistency on the golf course. We often give the following advice to golfers: "Practice how you intend to play." In other words, create conditions on the practice ground that simulate conditions in a competitive environment on the golf course. Satisfy yourself that you are doing all you can to achieve this goal.

Undoubtedly you have witnessed many golfers beating a bucket of balls with one or two clubs until they are satisfied with the outcome, though they are rarely satisfied. Although your coach might recommend such practice for a particular reason, this practice does not resemble the game of golf. Rarely do you use the same club twice, though there are occasions when we all have to!

The generous lie you give yourself each time on the practice range is not what it is like on the golf course. How often are you hitting shots from the rough or a downhill lie over a water hazard? Or how often are you hitting shots from a divot? These are all parts of the game that we find on the course but we may not find on the mat at a driving range. When we practice how we intend to play we are asking ourselves to be disciplined and focused. We do not mindlessly hit ball after ball; rather, we take our time to hit each ball towards a target as we would on the golf course.

We should look to create conditions similar to the course, in our mind, by telling ourselves that we are playing a competitive round of golf. We feel anxious because we are about to hit a shot to the green over the water to a tight pin. Ask yourself to remain committed to your target and focused on seeing a clear picture of the flight of the ball to the pin or to the fat part of the green. Take one minute to prepare, execute and evaluate each shot.

In one hour, you should have hit no more than sixty balls and the quality of your practice should resemble what you expect on the course. Remember that in golf you have to hit your ball and walk before you play your next shot so you should create a time difference between shots. Use this time to help yourself accept the outcome of your shot and prepare mentally to hit your next shot.

To play better golf, you need to practise as you intend to play. Arrange conditions in your practice routine to resemble conditions on the course. Give yourself enough time to prepare, execute, and evaluate each shot before preparing for your next shot.

Fault 2: Sometimes on the range, I cannot seem to hit a thing and, at other times, it just flows perfectly

How Common is the Fault  How Difficult to Fix

 Confidence is the most important single factor in this game, and no matter how great your natural talent, there is only one way to obtain and sustain it: work.

Jack Nicklaus

We, as human beings, are always trying to explain why things happen as they do. Most golfers would love to know why they play excellently on one day and play abysmally the next. The way in which we explain those things in our lives tells us about how optimistically or pessimistically we approach life. It makes sense to think optimistically about your life and how things will work out for the better. This same lesson applies when you are playing golf.

Some golfers feed a downward spiral when their practice session is not going to plan and their self-talk (i.e., what they say to themselves), is negative and derogatory. Can you think of such times? You might be saying "Oh, that was a lousy shot, can't you do anything right?" or "Just keep your eyes on the ball, how hard can that be? It's simple." The outcome of each shot frustrates you and, unfortunately, most of these comments serve to highlight our weaknesses. They make us think less about what we can do and more about what we cannot do! In short, we begin to focus on doing the opposite of what we intend to achieve.

To get into the flow of positive practice on the range you need to begin by planning your session. Ask yourself: "What are my goals today?" Once you have decided on your first goal, for example, to hit 60% of your wedge shots to within 10 yards of the pin; you can begin your practice. Remember, each shot should include a positive target (i.e., what you *want to do* rather than what you *want to avoid*) and a pre-shot routine. Once you have executed the shot, evaluate it and forget about it as you plan your next shot.

In your pre-shot routine, you can remind yourself that you are a capable golfer with statements such as: "With each shot I hit, I am becoming a better ball striker." Some golfers need to repeat this statement a few times before striking the ball. This statement is effective because it overrides our negative mental chatter with positive intention and support. This strategy of encouragement will help you get back into the flow of your swing – let your swing do its thing.

You are not asking yourself to hit a perfect shot or achieve a perfect outcome each time; rather you are telling yourself that you are a good ball striker and, with a positive approach to each shot, you can accept the outcome. What you cannot accept is sloppy preparation for each shot. Our aim is to create the feeling that we are able and capable of striking that little white ball and the outcome doesn't matter because we are focused on striking the ball well and we will deal with the next shot when we approach it. It doesn't make us happy or sad; it is just another shot to hit. The flow to our swing returns when we free ourselves enough to be athletic in our set-up. We can swing successfully because our body is not tight and rigid - worrying about not hitting a ball well. We are thinking only about hitting one shot at a time.

We get back to positive practice on the range by planning our session, adopting a pre-shot routine for each shot, encouraging ourselves, and accepting the outcome of each shot - whatever the result.

Fault 3: I hit hundreds of balls on the range but never seem to get much better

How Common
is the Fault

How Difficult
to Fix

 I don't know if it's sinking in but I've got to make the effort - and this is the big thing - to believe it, to accept it. Many times I've had these long discussions during evenings with friends of mine and my brothers about believing it as much as they do. I would sit there, sometimes paying lip service to what they were saying. But having won three majors in the modern era and looking at the players I can compare myself with, in terms of the majors they have won, I've got to start accepting that I am who I am.

Part of getting to the next level and achieving more sustainability, especially in normal tournaments, is believing that I am world No 3 at the moment and that I'm improving. But that is a genuine way of improving my game, coming to terms with it and having a little more of that free-flowing confidence. I need to turn up and say, 'I am the player here to watch'.

Padraig Harrington
speaking about having won three majors

We meet many golfers walking off the 18th green bewildered by their performance on the course and the scores on their card. They explain that they have spent hour after hour hitting balls on the range but they do not see their scores fall on the golf course. After a few brief questions, we usually uncover a logical explanation for the complaint. First, the time spent on the range is typically long and lazy rather than short and focused. They spend most of their practice time operating without a plan to improve. Second, because the sessions are long, they often adopt a sloppy routine before striking the ball. As one golfer put it, "When there's a basket full of balls and no one is keeping score then there's no consequence if I don't pay attention and play each shot well." Third, practice time does not resemble actual events on the golf course. For example, putting typically accounts for 40% of the strokes in golf so it makes sense that it should comprise 40% of your practice time. If 40% of your practice is not spent putting then you will not lower your score.

Setting and achieving goals is an effective psychological technique to build confidence, motivation and commitment to excel in golf. Our goals must challenge us each time we practise and play. It is sensible to keep your goals SMART. This acronym represents: Specific, Measurable, Action-oriented, Realistic, and Timetabled. You should keep a notebook in your golf bag for each practice session to allow you to write down two goals that relate to practice. For example, you first goal might be to spend 40% of practice time on the putting green, 30% with the short game, and 30% on the long game.

Your second goal might be to positively reinforce your effort during the session. You can reward yourself by using simple words of encouragement or instruction, "Well done, you focused on a low, smooth take-away." The aim of this goal-setting exercise is to create a positive motivational climate for your practice where you know that you have structured your practice around the appropriate aspects of the game, and you reward yourself for doing the right things well.

Practise with a purpose. Each practice session should include at least two goals that you aim to achieve in the short term and in the long term. Use your goals to challenge yourself. Reward yourself for your effort.

Fault 4: I slip into bad practice habits on the range

How Common
is the Fault

How Difficult
to Fix

> *Perhaps the truest test of a player is whether you can rise to the greatest of occasions. When you are on the course you have to be able to concentrate at the right times and to think clearly at the right times. But it starts even before you get to an event: you have to be able to take your game with you and raise it up for the occasion.*
>
> **Jack Nicklaus**

Practising on the range can be psychologically demanding because we receive feedback about each shot we make. This feedback comes from the movement of the ball (e.g., a draw or a hook) and its landing position (e.g., on or off target). Sometimes the ball goes where we want it to go but our technique was poor; at other times the ball goes where we did not intend it but we feel we hit it well. This feedback is demanding psychologically because we have to cope with the thoughts and emotions we experience after every shot. We force ourselves to explain why things happened as they did which drains us of our energy to practise well. Focus less on the outcome of each shot and focus more on whether you prepared yourself properly by following your pre-shot routine.

Although the driving range can help us to improve our golf game, it rarely penalises us for sloppy preparation or poor shots. If we hit a poor drive, we can simply tee up another ball and take the shot again. In some ways, the next ball helps us to forget about the last one. That is why we should practise on the range how we intend to play on the course but also have a checklist or a video camera to review our behaviour, every now and then. A video camera, for example, is useful to tell us how much time we take to prepare and execute a shot. It also tells us about our habits and how we react psychologically to our shots. Every few weeks, it would be useful to see your practice behaviour on camera.

It is important not to become too focused on making a perfect swing every time. The goal is to be athletic and free flowing in your movement; however, to be athletic and free flowing, we need to establish our own pre-shot routine and execute this routine for every shot we play. If you don't have a pre-shot routine you should develop one.

The value of a routine is that we can put ourselves into the right physical and mental set-up to ensure consistency. Most golfers lay clubs on the ground to make sure they are linking up correctly and it is excellent practice for all golfers. For 20% of the shots that you hit you should take the clubs away from the ground and try to go through your routine with just the image of the clubs on the ground. Get set up and when you are mentally ready to take your shot you can begin your movement. The aim of this practice is to help you forget about thinking in terms of technique all the time – you need to think about the target and focus only on the target for those shots.

You should not be too concerned with the outcome of each shot, especially if you are making changes to your swing. The most important part is that you commit to each shot. You must spend your time wisely on the range and develop a readiness to excel with these shots. The problem for most golfers is that they never spend any time after working a technical change to practise as if they were on the course. That is the true test of the golfer.

Quality on the range means quality on the course. Attend to your pre-shot routine and rest for a while when you feel you are not paying complete attention to the shot you are about to take.

Fault 5: I am slow to get going when I play on the course

How Common
is the Fault

How Difficult
to Fix

 Of course my confidence is not what it was. When you are winning Majors by big margins like I was in 2000 then you are riding a real high. Ask anyone out there and they will tell you there is no substitute for confidence. Everyone has his moments of doubt, but you have to overcome them. It's part of playing sport. You just have to get out there and believe in your ability. If you put in the work and know what you can do, it's a matter of going out there and executing it properly.

Tiger Woods

Getting up to speed on the golf course is often a reflection of your preparation for the game. What we mean by this statement is that you give your best when you are *best prepared* to give your best.

If you are getting to the course late with little time to warm up, it is unreasonable to ask too much of yourself for the first few holes until you relax, stretch, and get a feel for the greens and the conditions. Too many golfers expect themselves to adapt to the conditions immediately and if they do not, they get anxious and upset with how they are performing. A key aspect of performing well is to accept conditions as they are and accept your present circumstances.

Some golfers, even though they have been diligent in their practice and preparation before the round, still feel that it takes them some time to get started in the game. This often happens because the players do not have a plan for their game and they have come away from the driving range without having organised themselves for the first three holes. If you know the yardage for the first three holes you can finish your practice session on the range as if you are playing these holes. So, for example, with a 520-yard par 5, you might begin with a driver, followed by an iron and then a wedge to the green. You can then play the second hole, perhaps a par 3 and follow that hole with a short par 4 giving you a simulation of the first three holes you are about to play in on the course. This strategy helps you to prepare your mind for the shots you want to play.

When you play on the course, you might realise that what you had practised does not specifically map to what is happening, however, you have made the best plan based on your skills and ability, which prepares you to play with confidence and trust. When you don't have a plan, you can easily be distracted by a poor shot or indecision on which shot you should make. You can prepare yourself on the range for all eventualities so that if it happens on the course, you are still in control because you know exactly what to do next. The key is to plan your work and then work your plan.

Golf challenges us to be prepared for all eventualities. Leave the practice range with a clear plan for your first three holes.

Fault 6: I feel so nervous on the first tee and often hit a poor shot

How Common is the Fault		How Difficult to Fix	

> *I hit it so bad warming up today... I was hitting quick hooks, blocks, you name it. Then on the first hole, I almost hit it into the eighth fairway (across the ninth fairway and the members' practice area). It's one of the worst tee shots I've ever hit starting out. I fought my swing all day and just kind of Band-Aided it round.*

Tiger Woods

It is natural to feel nervous on the first tee. We feel nervous because the outcome of the shot is important to us, we are unsure about the outcome, and there is usually an audience watching us. Feeling nervous is our body's way of telling us that we are preparing for action and as Jack Nicklaus said, it is the "truest test" of a player to rise to the occasion. And that is one reason why so many golfers spend time on the practice range to prepare for the first tee. But if you think about it, this shot is no different from any of your other shots because each stroke counts.

We explained, earlier, that much of our practice time is wasted because the practice conditions do not resemble what we experience on the course. On the first tee you might have an audience, and you might feel that you have not prepared as well as you would have liked but you are forced to take a shot, often with a driver with obvious hazards. Many professional golfers also feel nervous on the first tee and many times they fail to execute the shot they were intending to execute. Remember the first tee of the 2006 Ryder Cup at the K-Club in County Kildare in Ireland? Tiger Woods drove it into the water. And if Tiger can do it, perhaps we should not be too hard on ourselves and expect too much.

When we lower our expectations, we naturally begin to relax and allow ourselves to play the game we are capable of playing. Nobody else is holding our club – we are in charge. If you accept that during a round of golf, it is normal to have poor shots, you can accept that one poor tee shot will not disrupt your game. It might be annoying but you can adapt and continue to play the game.

The key to hitting a good shot off the tee might depend on using your favourite club that suits you and gets you to play your best golf – how much better is the middle of the fairway compared with the rough? If you are comfortable hitting a six-iron or rescue club off the tee, then *have the confidence* to choose that shot – that is what a composed and confident golfer would do. If you watch golf on TV, the positive professional takes the best option for himself, or herself, every time.

No one else will play with your ball. It is your choice how you get it into the hole; so be sensible and do it the best way for you rather than what you think is best to match everybody else's opinions.

Fault 7: When I have a scorecard in my hand, I go to pieces

How Common
is the Fault

How Difficult
to Fix

 I have never done a better job of doing the things I do well for all 18 holes. It is the most boring thing in the world to say you have to take one shot at a time but it's what Tiger does and it's what Jack Nicklaus did.

Davis Love III
after a win at Sawgrass

Most golfers equate their scorecard with their school report. Perhaps it conjures up images of earlier school days with comments such as, "could do better" or "we expected more at this stage". In school, our teachers evaluated our academic performance. At home, our parents evaluated our social behaviour. In sport, our coaches evaluated our sport performances. These dominant learning experiences suggested that we ought to evaluate ourselves to assess how well we are doing relative to those around us. Unfortunately, many people have adopted poor strategies to evaluate their performances. For instance, success is absolute rather than relative. In other words, if I win (e.g., the tournament) I am a success. If I lose, I am a failure. This perspective does not account for different stages in one's career, whether one is returning from injury or whether the competition is appropriate for a player's current standing in the game.

Our challenge is to understand how we see success and failure in sport and life. Success for one person might be breaking 90 but for another person (who plays professional golf) breaking par is essential but realistic. Therefore, we ought to be realistic about our current playing ability. If you begin a round of golf by setting a score in your head, this number ought to be challenging but realistic for your current capability. The scorecard will accept any numbers you write on it and it will not ask you to draw a picture of how you scored par on a par 4. The problem for many golfers begins when they write a number to which they attach meaning. For example, scoring a five on a par 4 means a bogey for that hole, and some golfers will believe that bogeys are unacceptable.

A better strategy to approach your golf game would be to fill out your card the night or morning before you play. In this way, you can write in the numbers you feel are challenging but realistic on each hole without the emotion you naturally feel on the golf course. A birdie on a par 5 might be realistic and challenging for you whereas a par might be realistic and challenging for another golfer.

Be sure to consider the weather conditions and the stroke index of each hole. If you wish, you can plan each hole and how you would like to play them. For example, on a 320-yard par 4, you might write D, 9i, 2p on your scorecard (where D = driver, 9i = 9 iron, and p = putt). So regardless of your score on the previous hole, you have planned either the night or morning before what to do on the next hole. If things go wrong on one hole, it doesn't give you permission to give up, because *you* are in charge of your golf game. If you can play golf without attaching value to numbers, you will begin to play much better golf.

When Darren Clarke scored a round of 60 at the K-Club for the European Open, he wasn't even thinking about the score. He just played each hole, refrained from evaluating it, and moved on to the next one.

A scorecard is a device for recording your score. The scorecard will not determine how you intend to play – that choice is yours. Plan your round before you play and you'll enjoy holding that scorecard in your hand.

Fault 8: When I have a three-foot putt, I often miss them but I think I should score easily

---

How Common is the Fault   How Difficult to Fix

 I made the mistake about thinking which section of the crowd I was going to bow to! I had the victory speech prepared before the battle was over... I would give up every victory I had to have won that title. It's amazing how many different things in my normal routine I did on the 18th hole. There is something for psychologists there, the way that the final hole of a major championship can alter the way a man thinks.

Doug Sanders
at the final hole at St. Andrews with a
putt to win the 1970 British Open

Three-foot putts must be easy to score because they look like they are as close to the hole as they can be for a reasonable attempt at a putt. But three-foot putts and other putts in that short range can be difficult for lots of reasons. Do you remember the famous putt to win the British Open Championship in 1970? Doug Sanders had a short putt to win the Open but as you have read in the quote, his mind was focused on the victory speech and not on the putt.

Short putts are difficult for at least two reasons. First, because the ball is close to the hole, most golfers expect to score and believe that those watching them (e.g., playing partners and the gallery) also think they should score. Second, our memories of missed putts in this range flood back because our emotions are tied to these memories. So if we are feeling anxious, we recall instances when we felt anxious before - as well as the outcomes of events at that time. We can deal with each of these circumstances in turn.

The Successful Golfer

Our expectations of ourselves on the golf course change over time. Our expectations of ourselves even change *during* a round of golf. Such expectations are helpful, at times, to motivate ourselves to work hard at our game. If you believe you are a competent golfer, then you need to practise each element of your game to be what you believe you are – a competent golfer.

If, when we are on the golf course, we expect to roll a three-foot putt into the cup, then we ought to pay attention to our routine and think only about the needs of the putt. To prepare for this eventuality on the course, you ought to practise short putts in a stressful situation to mimic those conditions on the golf course. For instance, you might have a putting competition with a friend. To add more stress, you might compete for money. If you are practising on your own, you could try to imagine how you would feel preparing to stroke a four-foot putt to win the Masters at Augusta. Or give yourself the challenge of putting ten three-foot putts in a row; if you miss a putt, you must begin again until you successfully putt ten three-foot putts in a row. As you improve, you might practise to roll in 30 or 50 three-foot putts in a row.

Dealing with memories of poor performances is challenging but not an impossible difficulty to overcome. Trying to shut out these memories often hastens how quickly these memories return. A better strategy is to fill your mind with positive, action-oriented tasks that focus on the task at hand.

With a three-foot putt, you need to firstly read the line of the putt assessing, as best you can, the break around the hole. Once you have decided on the line of your putt, see the ball roll along that line and drop into the cup. Go through your routine and stroke the putt only when you have gone through each step of your routine diligently.

Each putt we stroke has as little or as much importance as we attach to it. Learn to treat each putt as if it has the same value. Then go through your routine and stroke your ball confidently to the hole.

Fault 9: I often end up short of the green when I know I should hit the green

How Common
is the Fault

How Difficult
to Fix

 Before Tiger came along, I worked just as hard as I work now. You try to find different things that you can work on in your game by looking at other people, but I've always worked hard.

Jim Furyk

Most golfers in the world suffer from positive illusions. What that means is that they are overly optimistic about their chances of executing a shot. Funnily enough, people are much better after doing a task at predicting how confident they are at the task!

On most golf courses the biggest trouble a golfer can encounter will be *in front* of the hole, which means that if you are short of the green you probably find yourself in trouble. So why are we reluctant to take an extra club? And why do we overestimate our distances?

Professional golfers hit up to 75% of greens in regulation in any season. Indeed if they do hit as many as 75% of the greens, they would consider themselves very capable of hitting the green. But remember that even when they are playing their best they miss the green on one in every four shots. When they are playing averagely, they might hit three out of five greens which means that on two occasions they will have to get up and down to save par.

Whilst we expect ourselves to do well, we don't always make good decisions and we are all affected by hindsight bias; after the shot we remark, "Oh what a pity, just an extra club and I would have been perfect." To avoid this situation, you need to be honest with yourself and give a candid estimation of the likelihood that you can hit the green with the club you are holding in your hand.

Good golf is a mental game but it is also a course management game and so both parts should work together to give you the best outcome for your efforts. Tom Watson recommends taking an extra club and swinging easy to the fat part of the green. And if Tom Watson thinks it's a good idea to do so perhaps we ought to listen to his advice.

Before you swing your club, ask yourself, what are my realistic chances of achieving the outcome I want here? When you have answered this question, aim for an even more conservative club selection.

Fault 10: I feel my body getting twitchy when I have to play a short wedge to the green

How Common
is the Fault

How Difficult
to Fix

 Expectations are very hard to deal with when you don't have the necessary skills to back them up. I think now I have a lot of trust in my game and I feel like if I put myself in a situation with a chance to win I have the tools at my disposal to enjoy the occasion and, for the very least, for it not to be overwhelming.

Justin Rose

The human body is an amazing machine. It is capable of many feats such as running ultra-marathons, climbing the world's highest mountains, and running 100 metres in under 10 seconds. It is also capable of hitting a short wedge to the green.

All of these achievements require practice to excel at the highest level. Motor skills, like those in golf (e.g., swinging a club), require practice to allow an individual to execute the shot without conscious control. Most of us could toss a golf ball to a friend without thinking about it – we see where our friend is standing and we toss the ball. We don't need to think about the angle of release or wind speed; we just see it and do it.

You might argue that tossing a ball is a relatively easy task unlike hitting a wedge shot to the green and you are right because there is much greater complexity in the latter task. The point here, however, is that if we have hit many, many wedge shots we instinctively know how to hit that ball to the green. The problem arises when we tell ourselves that we cannot do it. When we feel in our mind that we cannot achieve a set goal our body often reacts to this threatening information by increasing our heart rate and blood pressure and creating tension in our muscles.

31

The Successful Golfer

We feel this tension, which *reinforces* the thoughts we had about the threatening shot to the green.

To break this cycle, we need to learn how to relax physically as well as mentally. To relax physically, we can begin by breathing deeply and allowing each breath to reduce our heart rate. At the same time, we feel the tension being released from our muscles. To relax mentally, we need to gain control by reminding ourselves that we have executed this shot hundreds and thousands of times before. We then set about our pre-shot routine. This routine might comprise choosing the right club for the shot, imagining the ball landing on the green, focusing on the target and then back to the ball before taking your club away and executing the shot. Each golfer will have a different routine but what is most important is that the routine has been practised often, with a specific target, allowing you to feel a sense of control while you execute the shot.

Our mind and body are connected so we need to relax and gain control through our physical actions (e.g., taking deep breaths) and mental ones (e.g., reminding ourselves that we are capable of executing the shot).

Fault 11: If I have a poor drive, it ruins my score on the hole and the game

How Common
is the Fault

How Difficult
to Fix

   I don't have to hit perfect shots to make pars. It's [Augusta] not like the US Open where if you make one little mistake, it's costing you one or two shots because you don't have the ability to recover. I think that's what's exciting about Augusta National - the recovery shot.

Phil Mickelson

Many golfers put so much pressure on themselves to hit their drives perfectly that they often do the opposite of what they intended. Rather than hitting their drive onto the short grass, it ends up in the long grass. And because they hit a less than perfect drive, it somehow predicts their performance for the rest of the game. If one action was to influence another action so directly, one might also conclude that a failure to play with a *particular ball* will also lead to a poor game. Such superstitious thinking can, and does, hurt people's performances in golf as well as other sports. Such irrational thoughts do not help you to play your best golf.

You might well hit a poor drive, but that drive does not determine the outcome of the hole or game unfailingly. You haven't had a chance yet to hit your second shot and you cannot determine where it lands without hitting that shot. So you are better off leaving the crystal ball gazing to those who do it for a living – you are a golfer so it's time to deal with the present.

The challenge for most golfers is that they expect to hit the ball well but do not cope so well when the ball does not reach the target they expected. Many tour professionals only hit the fairway two-thirds of the time that they attempt to do so. In other words, only two of the three tee shots they hit actually land where they expected them to land. Where these professionals excel is in the recovery – the mental recovery. First, they accept that the ball has not landed on the target they expected. Then, they assess the specifics of their next shot to allow themselves the best chance to recover. Once they have made a decision, they get into their routine and execute the shot.

So what can we learn from the professional golfer? Perhaps the most important lesson to learn is that the golfers who make the fewest mistakes usually win golf competitions. Rather than viewing the poor drive as limiting their score, they look at the challenge of the next shot. They are keenly aware that golf is not a game of perfect drives – it is a game, and one to be enjoyed.

Playing good golf means that we ask ourselves: what is the challenge of my next shot? Regretting the outcome of the last shot wastes your time and steals your focus from the details of the next shot.

Fault 12: I often end up three-putting when I have a great chance of a birdie

How Common
is the Fault    How Difficult
to Fix

 Putting shouldn't be hard ... but that's where the mind comes in. So much running through your mind – hold it this way, keep the blade square – whereas when you're young, you just get hold of it and hit it. When you get old too much goes through your mind.

Ian Woosnam

When a golfer hits a good second shot to the green on a par 4, it's natural for the player to begin to think ahead. After all, most humans plan for the future. A schoolgirl might study at home each evening to ace her exams which then allow her to go to university. Golfers are similar in their thoughts about the future. They might start to think how a birdie chance will have a good effect on their current score; perhaps it 'makes up' for the bogey on the last hole. Alternatively, thoughts may be as simple as this 'birdie will look good on my scorecard.'

When a golfer starts to think in this way, they are 'thinking ahead' and focusing on things outside their control. When we think in this way, we begin to expect something of ourselves that directs our attention away from the task. So when the golfer sets up to stroke the putt, the golfer is thinking as Doug Sanders was thinking at the Open in 1970. The golfer is not focused on a routine and a trusted, smooth stroke. No, the golfer is thinking about how important this putt is to make that birdie, how sweet it will look on the scorecard, how it will propel the golfer onto playing better on the holes that follow.

But all these thoughts do not help you to play your best. You need to score *without* thinking about what each score means. The ball does not know the score and neither does your putter. It is only you, the golfer, who knows what the putt

35

means.

To address this circumstance, golfers need to avoid adding a value to each shot. Every shot in the game of golf is as valuable as the one that precedes it, or the one that follows it. So you can either choose to think that they all matter equally or they don't matter at all. Thinking about a 'birdie putt' means that we are thinking about the future rather than what we need to do right now to stroke the ball on the intended line towards the hole.

You need to get back to your routine, which helps you to forget about the outcome of the putt and what it means; allow yourself to go through the process and feel good about executing your putt. Trust your routine and your routine will let you play free and easy, with enjoyment. Remind yourself that you are in charge of your thoughts, feelings, and actions.

When you begin to think about the value of a putt, step back, focus on your breathing and get back into your routine.

Fault 13: Whenever I try not to think about hitting the ball in the water, that's exactly where it goes

How Common
is the Fault

How Difficult
to Fix

*I never hit a shot, not even in practice, without having
a very sharp, in focus picture of it in my head. It's like
a colour movie.*

Jack Nicklaus

Golf makes us think many different things, especially when the scores are tied and you're on the 18th fairway with a shot to the green. Get it close to the pin and you have a good chance for a birdie to win the competition but the water hazard to the left of the green makes the green look much smaller. The landing area becomes tighter and as you look down at the green the thought of not hitting the ball into the water starts to get stronger. So strong, in fact, that it is all you can think about, not hitting the ball into the water. In your mind's eye, you only see the ball dropping into the water. It's time to take the shot to the green but the image remains and you become a little tense as you get into position and make the shot. You strike the ball pretty well but as it is heading for the green it draws more and more until it drops into the water. As much you tried to hit that green, it wasn't going to happen. This is paradoxical because you got exactly what you were trying to avoid. This is what psychologists call ironic processing. Similarly, a rugby player might be thinking: "Don't drop the ball" as he waits for a pass from a team mate. He becomes so anxious thinking about not dropping the ball that when the ball arrives, he cannot catch it cleanly and drops the ball. He did exactly the opposite of what he intended.

Although you may have a persistent, negative thought in your mind, this thought does not have to disrupt what you intend to do. The more we try to suppress this thought, the more difficult it is to do so, and we tend to devote more mental resources to the suppression task rather than thinking about what we want to happen – striking the ball to the centre of the green.

To help you in this situation, you need to shift your focus toward something external like the back of the ball or a smooth take away of your club. This external focus (i.e., something in our environment but not in our head) helps us to attend to cues that are relevant to the shot (i.e., striking the ball) rather than cues that are irrelevant to the shot (i.e., the hazard around the hole).

Some golfers tell us about a particular tee shot on their home course that typically ends up in the trees or out of bounds. In this situation, for example, we advise golfers to focus on an external task relevant cue (e.g., smooth take away) as they practise this shot on the range.

Trying not to think about something happening is challenging for our minds. Our mind works best by giving it something to think about that is positive and relevant to the task at hand.

Fault 14: Even the slightest noise interrupts my concentration

How Common
is the Fault

How Difficult
to Fix

*I played an aggressive high-spinning pitch as routinely
as I have ever played a golf shot. I felt no emotion
standing over the ball. I could have been anywhere –
in the smallest tournament, on the practice ground or
in my back garden.*

Padraig Harrington
playing the 18th at the 2007 British Open
before he won

We have many distractions to deal with when we play golf. These distractions could be the weather, cheering crowds, mobile phones, people talking, and so on. There is no way we can control these distractions because most of them are caused by somebody or something else. And if these things are outside our control, we can only control ourselves, and how we react to these disruptions to our concentration. We cannot complain about them or allow them to upset us on the golf course because that one disruption will begin to fester and distract us from the shots that follow.

It is important to remember that noises around us do not cause us to lose our concentration, instead, we allow ourselves to *direct* our concentration away from cues that are relevant to the task. At golf tournaments, we should all be able to recall instances when golfers executed their shots despite noises from the crowd, flashing cameras, and mobile phones. On occasions when golfers allowed themselves to be distracted by the noise and struck the ball poorly, it is likely that they blamed the noise for their poor performance.

Unless we prepare for these challenges on the golf course, it is possible that distractions will hurt our performances. We can prepare for these challenges by creating practice conditions that challenge us to focus only on the needs of the task at hand. If we are distracted as we prepare for our shot, we can retake our pre-shot routine. We can ask a friend or coach to distract us on the practice range or putting green by making noises that are typical on the golf course. Your friend or coach should also aim to distract you when you least expect it to test how well you remain focused on the task at hand. Tiger Woods remarked that his father created distractions such as dropping a bag of clubs as he was about to play his shot and walking into his line of sight as he was preparing to putt during practice rounds. This adversity training was designed to prepare Tiger for such distractions during competitive golf.

If we are distracted in our routine, we can let the distraction pass and get back into the routine. On the practice range, a coach or friend can create distractions that test us to maintain our focus on the needs of the task at hand.

Fault 15: I can't seem to relax the night before a big tournament

How Common is the Fault

How Difficult to Fix

 Some days I wake up and I'm so nervous I cannot hold the fork steady at breakfast.

Lee Trevino
replying to fellow professional Tom Watson, when
asked if he ever got nervous playing golf

Competitions make most people feel uneasy. People feel uneasy because the outcome of the competition is important to them but they are unsure about how they will perform and whether they will win.

With events that occur in the future, some people will look forward to the competition and see it as a challenge but others will see the competition as a threat. It is often our mental activity that keeps us awake the night before a big tournament and if we do not have a way to relax our mind, then it is much harder to get to sleep.

If your mind is racing, you might be thinking many different things all at once: how will the competition finish? Will I play well? Will I win? Have I prepared well? Who will be watching me? In addition to these thoughts, you might also be thinking about personal issues unrelated to golf. All these thoughts and feelings do not help us to relax.

We can use different strategies to relax. These strategies can help us relax physically and mentally and include listening to calming music or a relaxation recording, breathing techniques, and writing down what is bothering us at the time. These strategies are useful because they help us to focus on physical and mental actions that give us a sense of control. For instance, writing down what is bothering us at the time is a useful strategy because once we have committed those worries to paper we know we can deal with them at another time. You might have various things to prepare before the competition but, rather than worrying about them, you have made a list to deal with them in the morning.

You should get into the habit of using different strategies to help you relax so that you have a way to get to sleep when you most need it. The long-term value in learning to relax can be used best when you practise relaxation strategies over time. Many golfers practise breathing strategies to help them relax and sleep well each night. In turn, these breathing strategies can also help you to relax during a competition.

Relaxation is a skill and if we practise relaxing we can use this skill to help us relax when we most need to de-stress. Practise breathing in for four seconds and breathing out for eight seconds before you hit each shot in practice.

Fault 16: I feel so nervous on the morning of a tournament and I don't know what to do

How Common
is the Fault

How Difficult
to Fix

 The wheels are going to come off every minute ... No, no, no. Don't you believe it. Just focus on what you have to do ... What shot do you want to hit here? ... I want to hit a solid drive, a touch of fade ... Fine good that's more like it ... Now, where exactly do you want to land it? ... left-side of the fairway.

Nick Faldo
expressing his doubts before beginning his final round
at the 1996 Masters

The morning of a tournament is a challenge for all sport performers and especially golfers who are hoping to play well.

Strangely, most people think that when they feel nervous, it is a feeling that means something is wrong, or what is going to happen is certain to be unfortunate. Rarely do we recognise the signs of nervousness for what they are. Our body is telling us that we are preparing to perform in an event that is meaningful to us but we interpret these feelings in certain ways. For example, when we feel butterflies in our stomach, we might assume that feeling means we will not perform well but all we need do is get the butterflies to fly in formation. At other times, we might feel our legs shaking a little fearful that they won't support us to strike the ball off the first tee. When Padraig Harrington was teeing off in the Ryder Cup in 2002, he said he could hardly see the ball on the tee because he was so nervous. Even the top professionals feel just like how we feel.

The challenge here is to remind ourselves that the feelings we experience when we are nervous are simply our body's preparation for the upcoming competition.

If we did not feel nervous, the competition would be meaningless to us and would likely prevent us from playing to our potential. We can gain more control in these situations by following a routine to use our time purposefully.

This routine is something you can develop and follow to prepare best for the upcoming competition. For example, you might begin with a light breakfast, then prepare your golf bag and clothes for the tournament. If you have to travel to the golf course by car, you can allow yourself enough time to travel to get there with time available to warm-up before you play. You might wish to practise your long game and then your short game before moving to the putting green. The most important feature of your preparation is to allow you to gain a sense of control by thinking and doing things that help you prepare best to perform in competition.

You ought to spend time preparing sensibly for competition rather than worrying about what might go wrong. Plan your morning and work through your plan methodically. The more you plan and practise your morning routine, the greater the sense of control you will feel before competition.

Fault 17: I give myself a really hard time if I don't hit a perfect shot every time

How Common
is the Fault

How Difficult
to Fix

> *I talk to Justin about mindfulness and self-awareness. Every man has an ego and the favourite playground for the ego in a male golfer is the long game. Three years ago, Justin would get frustrated and lose his temper. If I simplify the long game for him, then there is no more ego and he need not get frustrated. He can put his energy into what he should be doing next.*

Nick Bradley, Justin Rose's former golf coach

Striving for perfection is something most people aim for in different parts of their lives. Some people wish to keep their car or house in perfect condition. Others aim to complete business projects perfectly. In golf, some golfers need, or want, to hit a perfect shot each time they hit the golf ball. This need or want is unreasonable for several reasons but mainly because we are human beings performing skills that are difficult to execute in a changing environment. Striving for perfection is a laudable aim if we are practising *to improve* rather than demanding perfect outcomes from ourselves in everything we do.

You might not recognise the differences between these two perfectionists but they differ immensely. When we go all out for perfection, known as 'perfectionistic striving', we engage a state of mind associated with self-confidence, the hope of success, and good performance in competition. But when we have perfectionistic concerns, we get anxious about competition and can develop a fear of failure.

For some golfers, this anxiety and fear of failure seriously affects their performance in competition and their overall feelings of wellbeing.

The Successful Golfer

Perfectionistic striving is a healthy way to help us practise and play golf. We aim to execute shots to the best of our ability but we recognise that we are human and make mistakes. The more we practise, the more likely we are to reduce the number of mistakes we make when we play golf. We can learn to accept mistakes as information that helps us to practise and play better in competition.

It is reasonable to ask ourselves to work hard, pay attention and strive to improve. But we should also allow ourselves to make mistakes and accept these mistakes as a natural progression towards excellence. Your goals for yourself ought to be challenging, not impossible. Pencils have erasers and keyboards have backspace buttons to help us undo our mistakes. When we make a mistake in golf we can take a piece of paper to write down the mistake, learn a lesson from the mistake, and then throw the piece of paper in the bin.

Learn to accept yourself as a fallible person first, and then as a fallible golfer. This fallible golfer is allowed to make mistakes but he strives to give his best when he practises and competes. What is less acceptable is making the same mistakes again and again without taking steps to address them.

Fault 18: I lose motivation to train if I don't do well in a game at the weekend

How Common
is the Fault

How Difficult
to Fix

> " *I have a plateful to work on. Golf is fluid;*
> *it is always evolving, always changing.* "
>
> **Tiger Woods**

Competition is often the litmus test of our ability as golfers. We do, however, retain the choice to determine how competition affects us, especially our motivation to continue striving to be our best. Sometimes competitions show a reflection of us, as golfers, that we would rather not see. Often that reflection is inaccurate (e.g., I always play poorly in competition) or accurate only for a little while (e.g., I have practised as much recently as I normally do), on a particular day (e.g., course conditions were difficult today), or on a particular weekend (e.g., I lost focus after playing well in the first round) – *not forever*.

In other words, a poor performance on one day does not determine the quality of the performances that follows. If we do perform poorly in a competition, we can assess that performance rationally and ask relevant questions: Did I prepare properly for the competition? How was I feeling before I began? What was I thinking during the competition? Did I trust myself and play athletically?

There are many ways to explain when someone has lost motivation to train because various factors are involved in this construct. A player may be returning from injury or has practised so much that they are physically and mentally tired from the game or their job. It is important to be reasonable with yourself when you assess your motivation to practise. If, however, we avoid practising because we do not want to experience more poor golf, then we can change that situation.

The Successful Golfer

First, you should plan your session so that it is short, sharp and focused rather than long and lazy. Write down what you intend to do and how long it will take you to complete the task. You might work on your short game for 40 minutes and spend 20 minutes on your long game.

Second, within this session, you can set targets that build a diet of success into your practice. A diet of success means that you ensure you show that you are competent at a skill by executing less difficult tasks before you tackle more difficult tasks. While putting, you could begin with two foot putts and listen to the ball drop into the hole; then you could move to three foot putts and so on. Remember to fair to yourself and do not expect perfection.

Finally, reward yourself. You might say "Good effort here, well done," or "You kept your focus during those challenging chip shots to the tight pin," or "I accepted the outcome of each drive and prepared properly with my routine for the next drive."

A competition is one instance in our sporting life – we should not allow one competition to determine what we think and feel about ourselves. Be fair on yourself and allow yourself to let go of poor performances but promise yourself to learn from each competition.

Fault 19: I can't seem to control my emotions when I get angry

How Common is the Fault		How Difficult to Fix	

 We know Darren's been prone in the past to completely losing his head. 'I told him that he had to accept the bad shots the same as he accepted great shots. Ben Hogan used to always say he would hit only five good shots a round. Darren wants to hit 99 percent of his shots perfect.

Mark McNulty
talking about Darren Clarke

Golf brings out many emotions; ecstasy when we win or stroke a great putt for an eagle, agony when we miss a putt to make the cut or win a tournament and anger when we demand much more of our golf game when we need it most and we fail to deliver.

Anger is an emotion we experience in golf especially when we aim to achieve a goal but do not realise this goal. Some people become frustrated because they were prevented from achieving a goal they set for themselves. For example, you might drive off in the first three holes and find the rough each time with the third time causing you to react angrily to the outcome of the shot. Your frustration may have grown because you recognise how often this happens in competitions that matter to you. Being frustrated or angry is only an issue for a golfer if it affects a golfer's performance negatively. Some golfers can cope with such emotions but it is an unwelcome emotional mix for others.

To the extent that you know yourself, especially how you think and feel on the golf course, we can begin to recognise what emotions you typically experience during the game and what triggers these emotions. You might hit a poor pitch shot and think, "Here we go again – I've dropped a shot on this easy par 5." These thoughts relate to a belief you have about yourself that ought to be challenged. You might over-generalise these thoughts and believe that one poor shot means a poor round of golf because it has happened before; however, if you allow yourself to consider those times when you did hit a poor chip shot and played a good round of golf you can challenge these self-defeating ways of thinking, feeling and behaving.

Getting to know what we believe and feel about ourselves as golfers helps us to address faulty thinking on and off the golf course. If you think about a belief you have that affects your game (e.g., I can't putt well from 4 feet), you can challenge this belief and remind yourself of those times you have putted well from 4 feet.

Second, if your belief persists, you can practise your putting from that distance to challenge your belief and build your confidence in your ability to hole those putts. From a motivational perspective, you might find yourself using the outcome of each shot to determine your worth as a golfer and a person: "A good shot means I am a good golfer and a good person whereas a bad shot means I am a bad golfer and a bad person." You are linking the outcome of an event to your self-worth rather than seeing the events for what they are – shots in a game of golf. Allow yourself the courtesy to strive to do your best but give yourself a chance to make mistakes without evaluating yourself in the process.

To release anger in the moment, you can engage in different physical actions such as stretching the fingers of each hand backwards, squeezing the towel you use to clean your clubs, or simply smiling to yourself for getting angry. Some golfers who get angry after mishitting a shot out of thick rough find it useful to walk seven or eight paces away from the ball and then return more calmly to take the shot again.

Getting angry triggers other thoughts and feelings that steal our focus for the game. Learn to accept the outcome of each shot – after all you cannot change the outcome … you can only prepare yourself to do your best on the next shot.

Fault 20: My game falls apart when I am in contention to win

How Common
is the Fault

How Difficult
to Fix

 I have a big picture outlook ... I am willing to fall, and I understand that it's OK to fall, but I am going to get back up. I may take a step back, but in the end I am going to take a giant leap forward.

Tiger Woods

One of the most intriguing things about the golf games of top golfers is their ability to get ahead and stay ahead when the competition matters most. Tiger Woods illustrates this ability perhaps more than any other golfer. But what could explain poor performance at the time when the golfer most needs to be at her best? Unquestionably, top golfers win because of their mental capacity to cope under pressure – they know what winning means and what it *might* mean for them; however, they give themselves an opportunity to continue doing what they know makes sense. They will continue with their routine, staying focused on the needs of the shot only, and accepting the outcome before preparing to play the next shot.

It sounds reasonably straightforward to strike the ball well, deal with the outcome of each shot without judging one's ability as a golfer, and continue to remain focused on the present. Yet, it is incredibly challenging for many golfers. One of the reasons it is so challenging is that the golfer has not practised this process well enough, for long enough, in conditions that resemble those on the back nine of a meaningful competition.

Although it is difficult to create those exact conditions in practice, we can at least try to simulate those conditions as best we can. For instance, imagine hitting as many four-foot putts in a row as possible. This task is challenging but there is no specific target. If we add a target of 40 three-foot putts in a row that we must make before we can go home from practice, we are putting ourselves under pressure. Think about how you might be feeling or what you might be thinking when you have holed 37 three-foot putts in a row and you have three balls left to putt. If you miss one putt, you have to go back to the start again and you might not want to begin again. As you get close to your goal, you challenge yourself to stay focused on stroking the putt only, and not on the meaning of the putt.

Remain focused only on what you can control and that is getting into your routine, trusting yourself, and accepting the outcome of each shot. Put each element of your golf game under pressure while you practise.

Fault 21: I never seem to live up to my expectations

How Common
is the Fault

How Difficult
to Fix

 The biggest thing for me is not the money, not the fame, any of that stuff. I just want to win. I enjoy winning; I enjoy competing on the biggest stage against the biggest players in the world. I think that's fun, that's what gets me off compared to having a lot of money, having everything in the world.

Jason Day

When you look in the mirror, do you appreciate and value yourself simply for being you? Or do you see someone you can only appreciate and value if that person has been successful in the eyes of others? For example, you might feel: "I like me when I win but I don't like me when I lose." When we tie our value as a person to objective outcomes like winning and losing, we begin to undermine our self-worth because our worth depends on success and failure – these things are often outside our control. And because they are outside our control and change often, we lose stability in the value we place upon ourselves.

It would be much better to value yourself as a person whom you like regardless of success or failure. You might choose to value honesty, loyalty, hard work, and commitment; each day you strive towards these goals but occasions when you are dishonest or disloyal ought not to undermine your sense of self. You are a human being and therefore, fallible. But you strive to give your best as often as you can. You know that you didn't wish to drive the ball into the rough or miss a three-foot putt. These things happen in golf and it is our choice to accept them and continually strive to improve. In the end, success and failure take care of themselves while you remain a person whom you like when you look in the mirror.

The Successful Golfer

Golf allows us many opportunities to succeed and fail in objective terms. But it also allows us the opportunity to test our commitment to do our best and our resolve to strive to improve. When we set our expectations to values within our control, we gain personal control and self-respect. You can live up to your expectations of commitment and trust, for instance, and still strive to win.

Sometimes our expectations are not realistic or fair on ourselves. We need first to be realistic and second to accept what we achieve while we strive to become better. For all our golfing lives, we are striving to become the best we can be. But at times we must take stock of where we are and as Shakespeare wrote, "To thine ownself, be true."

When we are honest with ourselves, we can begin to accept ourselves more. In turn, we can be happy for just being ourselves (without our achievements showing others *what* we are). A strong sense of self is the best starting point for any golfer.

Our advice to you is to learn to accept yourself for being you. Let your achievements take care of themselves. As Tiger Woods said, "Top golfers enjoy the serenity and challenge of competing against ourselves" rather than focusing on competing against others.

Accept yourself as a person first. A person whose worth does not depend on winning, losing or a crisply struck long iron to a tight green. Then, and only then, can you be successful.

Fault 22: I can't seem to concentrate when I have made a mistake

How Common is the Fault    How Difficult to Fix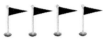

 At the Barclays Singapore Open last November (2008), I finished second and received lots of compliments. But when I thought about it I realised I'd had a four-foot putt to get into a playoff. There was no adrenalin in me, no intensity. The simple answer is I was so upset I had got a bad break earlier in the round that I was feeling sorry for myself. I got out of my routine, out of my zone, and I choked.

Padraig Harrington

Making mistakes is part of life. They allow us to get better at what we do, but only when we learn from them. You might have heard some people define madness as, "doing the same thing over and over again, and expecting the same result," and we are all guilty of some madness from time to time. The downward spiral of someone's game can follow a mistake but only if the golfer, allows it.

For some people, when they make a mistake they regret that mistake. The mistake might be selecting an 8-iron and coming up short of the green when a 7-iron would have carried your ball ten yards further to the pin. If you walk up to your ball regretting not choosing the 7-iron, you are focused on the past, not on what you need to do to chip, or putt, the ball close to the pin or into the hole.

Letting go of the past is challenging but not impossible. With practice, we can create a way to let go of what has happened and plan for what happens next. Whatever we do on the golf course – a good drive or a poor iron shot – is something we can acknowledge and accept because we cannot change the outcome. We can only focus upon what we want to think and feel. Our focus should be on preparing ourselves mentally to play the shot to the best of our ability. What happens after the ball leaves the face of the club or putter is something we can learn to accept.

Spend time on the practice range learning to accept the outcome of each shot – regardless of whether it was what you intended to do or not. Rather than valuing yourself when the shot goes the way you want and devaluing yourself when it doesn't, allow those thoughts and feelings to pass without attaching value to them. Then, prepare yourself for the next shot by focusing only on the demands of the shot. You might learn to place the outcome of the shot in your bag when you place your club back in there after the shot. Then, you plan for the next shot, when you take out your next club.

We ought to practise "letting go" of the outcome of each shot whether successful or unsuccessful. Each time we take the next club out of our bag we are playing as if there is no past and no future, just the present.

Fault 23: I can't putt well when I am nervous

How Common
is the Fault

How Difficult
to Fix

> *At no time did I even consider the mechanics of the stroke. Of course, I knew what the putt meant and what it was for, but I became absorbed in the line of the putt. I could see it exactly from beginning to end. My only job at that moment in time was to set the ball off on the line that I had chosen. That was the only thing I could control.*

Paul McGinley
on the putt to win the 2002 Ryder Cup

Putting for many people is an art. Something personal with many different strategies to roll the ball into the hole and it doesn't matter how you do it. You might putt with your right-hand below the left, left-hand below the right, or use a claw grip. You can even use a belly putter or broom handle putter - it doesn't matter.

Some golfers like to use a putter that is anchored to the body because their nervous feelings interfere with the motion of their putter head. Nervous feelings are usually physical. Your hands might shake a little, your legs might feel weak, or you might have a dry mouth. Add to those physical feelings some thoughts about what you want to happen and what the putt means on your scorecard.

There is nothing particularly wrong with these feelings; rather, the important thing is *what* you think about them. If you think these feelings will not help you putt well, then it is likely that you will not putt to your best.

When we learn to interpret such feelings as helpful and a natural part of what it feels like to do something that matters to us when the outcome is uncertain, we learn to perform well even with these feelings. It would be a good idea to create conditions that produce these feelings on the practice range. You might recreate the feelings that you experience on the golf course by having a competition with a friend, or creating a task for yourself that requires you to do the same chip shot 10 times in a row. For example, you might aim to hit 10 chip shots within 5 feet of the pin in a row. If you do not land all 10 chip shots within 5 feet of the pin, you must go back to the beginning and start again.

As you get closer to your target, you will probably feel nervous because you are getting close to your target and you might not want to start off again at chip shot number 1. As you get closer to your target, remember to breathe deeply to give yourself something to focus upon. Let your breathing relax your body – then begin your chip shot.

Our bodies help us prepare for action. We can learn to control our breathing to relax our bodies and interpret nervous feelings positively for putting.

Fault 24: When I putt, I always seem to leave the ball short of the hole

How Common
is the Fault

How Difficult
to Fix

 I was shaking on that putt and was shaking on a couple of them earlier.

Ernie Els
explaining how nervous he was feeling in the final
round before he won the 2002 British Open

Every skill in golf has mental and physical components. Most golfers emphasise the physical elements with less time devoted to the mental elements. Sometimes, a golfer's emphasis should be upon rectifying issues with stroke mechanics and these issues require time and instruction from a teaching professional. If you have developed sound mechanics with your putting and you still come up short of the hole, it is likely that you trust yourself less than you ought to.

There are two points to discuss here. First, you might think that you 'always' come up short of the hole but this impression of your putting might result from a decision-making bias. Simply, when a putt comes up short, it confirms in your mind that all your putts come up short. This is an example of confirmation bias. This may not be what actually happens with your putting! If after a rational analysis of your putting statistics, however, you feel your putts still come up short of the hole, then we can address the issue.

Second, as human beings, we tend to judge future events poorly such as how we will feel, what we will think about something, or what we will do. To the extent that this is true, it's best to adopt a more aggressive approach to our putting. For instance, golf commentators often mention putts falling below the hole (or on the amateur side) and putts going above the hole (or on the professional side) because amateurs underestimate the break on a putt more than professionals. Professionals also underestimate the break on putts but less than amateurs. The point here is that we all ought to overestimate the break on a putt.

If we are stroking putts tentatively, rather than confidently, not only does it highlight fear rather than trust in our putting but also it suggests that we underestimate the distance the ball will travel. To address this circumstance, we ought to practise overestimating the distance to the hole. If there is 10 feet to the hole, focus upon a point two feet beyond the hole (allowing for undulations on the putting surface) where you intend the ball to drop. This strategy will help you to trust the distance you intend to stroke your putt. A similar strategy is recommended for putting uphill to persuade golfers to stroke the ball with purpose.

A positive, athletic putting stroke illustrates your trust in your putting skills. Aim to overestimate the break and distance on various putts.

Fault 25: I have lost my confidence in golf

How Common
is the Fault

How Difficult
to Fix

 *I like a classic look, an old look for my driver. I don't
want too round a face. I want nice, smooth lines and
even if the clubhead is big, I don't want it looking big
and bulky. Golf's such a mental game that you've got
to be looking down on a club you like.*

Retief Goosen

Confidence is our belief in our ability, and expectations about achieving success based on those abilities. When we lose our confidence, we lose our belief in our ability and we do not expect to succeed in the challenges we set ourselves. These challenges might be to hole out a three-foot putt or drive a ball straight off the tee down the fairway.

Although someone might declare: "I have lost my confidence," it is often that the golfer has lost confidence in one or a few elements of the game. For instance, it might be driving or pitching, while bunker play and chipping is affected less. Because driving and putting are vital elements of the game, it might appear more devastating than is usual.

The first analysis a golfer should make is to assess whether this "loss of confidence" is a general or specific loss of confidence. Once this assessment is made, the golfer can begin to address their lack of confidence. Losing one's confidence is often about dealing with thoughts in our heads that influence what we think and feel. We learn to convince ourselves that what we could do before, we cannot do now.

To build confidence, we should set goals that are moderately challenging at first to provide a diet of success; then we can increase the challenges we set ourselves. We can also raise our confidence by encouraging ourselves with positive instructions, rewarding ourselves, preparing emotionally for competition and imagining success with our skills.

Confidence is about doing – so we must begin working on whatever task we want to improve upon. Though you might not feel confident, you can still pretend to be confident. You can walk and act as though you are confident which engenders and augments feelings of confidence. Tiger Woods, regardless of how his game is going, holds himself with an air of confidence that separates him from other golfers. One simple strategy to act your way into a confident feeling is to imagine you are being filmed for a golf advert. The director shooting the advert doesn't mind where the golf ball goes because she will film the ball landing by the pin afterwards. She just wants the golfer to act confidently before, during, and after striking the ball.

Our confidence depends on what we think, feel and do. We must continue to believe that we are capable and able to achieve the goals we set for ourselves. We must continually work to achieve our goals, imagine ourselves being successful, and encourage ourselves to remain focused on achieving our goals.

Fault 26: I lose my confidence if I start a game badly

How Common
is the Fault

How Difficult
to Fix

 Before I thought I could compete, now I know I can. There is a big difference.

Darren Clarke
after beating the World No. 1, Tiger Woods in the
World Match play in San Diego in 2000

We wrote already that confidence is our belief in our ability, and expectations about achieving success based on those abilities. Confidence, therefore, is based on the strength of that belief in the face of changing circumstances in the game of golf.

One of the challenges many golfers encounter is distorted thinking. Here are some examples:

- catastrophizing belief: the event that happened is absolutely awful or if it had have happened, it would have been absolutely awful
- intolerance belief: the event that happened is absolutely intolerable and I cannot cope with it
- self-deprecation as a core belief: the event that happened showed me or those who witnessed it that I am a useless and worthless human being

These evaluations lead to emotional distress and are unfair and disputable judgments one makes on oneself. For example, a poor drive on the first tee or a three-putt on the first green does not mean you are absolutely awful. It might be unwelcome or upsetting, naturally. However, you have the opportunity to prepare for each shot regardless of what just happened. You have the opportunity to dispute the assumption that you are a 'worthless human being' because all humans make mistakes. They learn to recover and learn from mistakes.

If you begin poorly, remember that you have the opportunity to think well of yourself and your golf game. You have the opportunity to dispute these false assumptions about yourself and how awful something might be. You have the opportunity to use your pre-shot routine to prepare and execute the shots that follow.

Your performance on one hole will only dampen your confidence if you allow it to determine how you react to your next hole. Remember to remind yourself that you are a worthy human being who understands that mistakes are part of learning and improving.

Fault 27: I lose confidence in parts of my game

How Common
is the Fault

How Difficult
to Fix

> **"** *Michael Campbell said that there would be small voices inside telling him "You've got to beat Monty", but that he would be doing his best to hit them on the head. "There's going to be a lot of self-affirmation going on. I will be talking to myself all the while and saying, 'I'm good enough to win'.* **"**

Michael Campbell

Although you might be a confident golfer, you might, at times, feel confident only in certain parts of your game. For example, you might be a confident driver of the ball and great with your irons but you might struggle on the greens, or you putt well but can't hit well with your driver.

As we have written already, our confidence is our belief in our ability to achieve our goals. But we only achieve our goals by doing, we need to be active and continue to practice our skills. But that alone is not enough if we undermine our ability by our mental chatter. That is, we tell ourselves we are not able, we cannot strike this ball off the tee; we know where it is going before we hit it and that is not where we want it to go. And here is where we have to be disciplined with ourselves and not allow ourselves to self-talk in a way that undermines our good feelings.

Another reason golfers lose confidence in parts of their games is that their practice time does not match their requirements on the course. Many golfers like to practise the skills at which they excel because it offers them good feelings about their game. Unfortunately, golfers fall into the trap of thinking they are competent and confident. We all need to gain a level of competence within our game, to allow us to excel on the golf course. For example, we might need much more time practising in the bunker than practising long-iron shots on the range.

The Successful Golfer

What we suggest is that you devote as much time as you can to those elements of the game that raise your competence as a skill - which will allow you to be confident under pressure on the golf course. We all know how important the short game is to lower your score and win at golf. Let's put that advice to good use and spend more time chipping, pitching, and putting our way to success.

We ought to develop competence in our skills to gain confidence when we need it on the course. Spend time practising those skills that are most necessary for you to play well, consistently.

Fault 28: I can't seem to play well for the big games

How Common is the Fault

How Difficult to Fix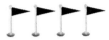

 You also have to be loose to play decent golf ... You can't believe how tense amateurs get playing in pro-ams. They're smart guys usually, but somehow they get it into their heads that they've got to impress the pro they're playing with.
Trust me, save your strength.

John Daly

The sports world is replete with examples of talented athletes who either didn't make it to a professional level or who made it briefly before failing. We may never know the exact reasons why one person succeeds in professional or elite sport and another does not, but it seems a pity if someone has the talent to compete in elite sport but perhaps lacks some specific guidance.

The desire to win is within us all but the will to win must be learned. For example, Gary Player recalled arriving for his first British Open in 1955: "I slept in the dunes. I wanted to win so badly." A sport professional can help develop skills and abilities within the golfer, which means that his or her career in professional sport is a reality, not just a dream.

When a golfer consistently performs poorly in games that are important, we can begin to understand how the golfer thinks, feels and behaves to explain the poor performances. In this situation, a golfer might think automatically 'I am going to play poorly today' because the golfer has learned that she does not play well in competitions that matter to her. Underneath this quick evaluation might be the belief that "If I fail today, I am a failure" and the core belief upon which this notion is built is that the golfer believes "I am a failure". The golfer needs support to dispute these beliefs and to replace them with more favourable beliefs that are not so self-destructive and demeaning. To the extent that this belief is persistent, more time is required to change this self-defeating belief to a more self-enhancing belief.

As well as playing golf, golfers also do other things too (e.g., work) and fulfil other roles as parents, siblings, and friends. Their lives outside sport might not present them with a chance to change how they feel about themselves so it requires even greater effort and discipline to treat oneself well regardless of whether one is on the golf course or not.

If you experience a self-defeating belief, before an important competition, you can write down three pieces of evidence to dispute this belief. For example, you could recall times when you played well when it mattered most to you. You could question whether it *always* happens or it just happens *sometimes*. You could remind yourself of the skills you have to play well. You could ask yourself whether it would be absolutely awful if you played poorly or just disappointing.

We should pay attention to our thoughts when we prepare and play on the 'big occasion'. If we are criticising ourselves unfairly, we ought to make a commitment to find two good things to say about ourselves (e.g., I work hard; I am a good person).

Fault 29: I drift in and out of the game

How Common
is the Fault

How Difficult
to Fix

*All that matters is that I have time to
prepare for the shot.*

Tiger Woods
on how he can play in silence or
talk all the way around the course

Many golfers feel that they drift in and out of games. Good periods of play are
followed by poor periods of play. You might begin with an excellent drive
followed by an accurate iron shot to the green and a 10-foot putt for birdie. And
that form might stay with you for four more holes. The next five or six holes you
find yourself struggling to make par or bogey. Nothing seems to have changed
with the difficultly of the holes but the poor form is difficult to shake off. Playing
well and playing poorly does not appear to be related to any physical changes in
swinging the clubs; rather, it seems that what the golfer is thinking and feeling
hampers the chances of recording a good round of golf.

In this situation, it is one's self-image as a golfer that is questioned. If you see
yourself as a competent golfer, you expect yourself to continue playing well
when you are playing well. When you are playing poorly, you expect yourself to
turn around the situation quickly and play golf competently and confidently as
you usually do. If, however, you hold a negative self-image of yourself as a
golfer, you will begin to undermine your periods of good play with thoughts such
as "I don't normally play this well, it's about to go all wrong for me" or "I have
to try to keep this going so don't hit this shot off line". Rather than accepting
your good play as a reflection of your competence as a golfer and the hard work
you put in to improve, you take every opportunity to place rigid demands upon
yourself. When the golfer with a poor self-image is playing well, he begins to
worry that it is all going to go wrong which fulfils his prophecy and he slumps
for a few holes. At the point of futility, he starts to let go of the demands upon

himself and suddenly, he picks himself up again and finishes the game well.

There is a lesson to learn here. First, all golfers should build a strong self-image by reminding themselves of their strengths. They should encourage and reward themselves for their efforts. They should soak up all the positive things people say about them and let go of all the negative things people say about them. They should pay attention to advice from a trusted professional about their game. Second, they must learn to play golf in the present. Playing in the present means focusing on each aspect of each shot only, nothing more. The consequence of what happens to your scorecard because of a birdie or four pars in a row does not matter. The score takes care of itself as long as you take care of living in the present.

We drift in and out of game when we do not play in the present. Your challenge is to focus on each shot only – one shot at a time. You don't need to evaluate what each shot means or whether good play will be followed by poor play.

Fault 30: I never play well when someone important is watching me

How Common
is the Fault

How Difficult
to Fix

 I am shy and reserved and that seems to go with my game. I try not to 'see' people when I am playing, because if I start reacting to them I'm losing my concentration.

Retief Goosen

For many golfers, the presence of a parent, coach or friend seems to be associated with poor performances on the course. These golfers erroneously believe that the presence of their parent, coach or friend is the reason why they do not play well. In some circumstances, critical parents might not be aware how judgmental and evaluative they are when they talk about golf with their child. And this can be a problem because the child knows that he or she will be evaluated regardless of how s/he plays which creates anxiety because the child cannot control what is being said about him or her.

Older golfers might have developed more resources to cope with evaluations; however, this is not always the case and, sometimes, their coping strategies become dysfunctional because they are hurt by the feedback. If we cannot control the environment around us, such as who attends the golf games we play, then we ought to explore why we feel the presence of particular people disrupts our performance.

At the core of this issue is a distorted thought pattern about the presence of others. For example, the presence of a parent can generate anxiety which disrupts performance. The belief at the core of this issue is that the child might feel that he has to play excellently, always, to show his father he is not worthless. Anxiety is typically dysfunctional and leads people to avoid threatening situations. Showing concern is a functional emotion that helps us to approach the threat appropriately. In a similar way, shame is a dysfunctional emotion that prompts people to hide away from others where s disappointment is functional and leads us to face up to others.

A golfer can create a rational dialogue to explore this situation. For instance, "I do not like it when my father comes to see me play because I feel anxious about being evaluated. He may annoy me by the things he says afterwards but I do not have to be annoyed by these things – they are not awful and I can tolerate them. With each shot I take in practice, I can learn to focus on each shot regardless of who is watching me. I value my father's opinion but I do not need his approval at all times to play my best golf. I know he just wants me to do my best."

We have no control over who turns up to watch us play or what they say about us. It is up to us to seek functional emotions, and ways of thinking, which help us to behave functionally and learn from our experiences.

Fault 31: I never seem to play as good as my friend, even though I am better

How Common
is the Fault

How Difficult
to Fix

 He's 22 years old and he's got a great attitude to the game. Rory's attitude and the way he carries himself on the golf course is the way everyone should try to be. He's got that bounce in his step. It's easy to bounce around the golf course when you hit it like he does.

Graeme McDowell
talking about Rory McIlroy

The first question to ask yourself is: how do you know you are better? And what exactly leads you to this conclusion? Once you can answer this question you can begin to understand the differences between you and whomever you are comparing yourself with. If, for example, you feel that an elegant swing or good equipment ought to be associated with a low score, then you should think about some successful golfers on the professional tours whose swings lack the elegance of others. Jim Furyk's swing might contrast with Luke Donald's swing – yet they are both highly accomplished golfers.

There is a good lesson to learn here. An elegant swing, although desirable, is not essential to scoring a low round in golf. Unstylish golfers can be effective when they find a way of getting the ball in the hole in fewer shots than others. In ball striking, the clubface is square at contact and they trust what they do implicitly. It's likely that their short game is the strongest part of their game. And vitally, they do not mind how they look to others; they are focused on trusting what they do. Golfers who are satisfied and happy with themselves as people, will not be concerned about how they look; they accept themselves as they are – no quibbles.

The key challenges for you are to (1) establish exactly where your friend makes his or her scores. If her short game saves her shots and you lose them, then your practice ought to focus on the short game. When you say you are better, find out exactly what you think you are better at. (2) Learn to accept yourself as you are. If you can say that you like yourself and you're happy with yourself regardless of how you play golf, you'll learn to overcome the emotional rollercoaster that golf can become – happy when you hit the ball well and disgusted when you hit the ball poorly.

You must believe that regardless of your swing and the clubs you have in your bag, the key factor is how well you get the ball from tee to green and into the hole. Forget the looks and think about the reality.

Fault 32: I can't stop thinking about playing badly before the game begins

How Common
is the Fault

How Difficult
to Fix

 *It was different in the past, but I've learned to get over
things pretty quickly. I genuinely don't care too much
if I miss a putt to win a tournament because I know
that I gave it my all.*

Retief Goosen

If you are standing on the putting green or on the driving range before you head
for the first tee and you're consumed with negative thoughts about how your day
is going to go, then you are preparing yourself for a challenging day.

When you think badly of your prospects, you unwittingly head directly for that
outcome. In psychology, this phenomenon is known as a self-fulfilling prophecy
and it means that we think, feel and act in ways that fulfil the prophecy we make.
If you think you are not a good golfer, then you act in every way to reinforce that
you are not a good golfer. If you think you are a bad bunker player, then you are
most likely to perform poorly when you step in there.

Most golfers forget that they can choose how they want to feel and what they
want to think and therefore how they want to behave. In their minds, they can't
change what they think, feel and do - but this is a faulty assumption. One of the
reasons why golfers feel this way is because they have not practised thinking,
feeling and behaving differently or they may have tried but *not persisted* to think,
feel, and behave differently. What we suggest here is that you ought to give
yourself at least eight weeks practising the change you want to make. If, for
example, you wish to think more positively on the golf course, you ought to
practise accepting the outcomes of each shot positively and rewarding yourself
for your effort. You need to do this for at least eight weeks before you see a

change in your thinking and therefore a change in your behaviour. If you intend to build a pre-shot routine, then you should spend your time on the practice range or the golf course practising this new pre-shot routine.

Each time you are about to think, feel or do something that is contrary to what you want to achieve, ask yourself one question: Will this (thought, feeling or action) take me towards or away from what I want to achieve? This simple question will prompt you to choose wisely.

Fault 33: I can't seem to get mistakes out of my head

How Common
is the Fault

How Difficult
to Fix

 *You can't be great at anything unless you explore it
right to the edge and if you're going to the edge,
mistakes will definitely follow. That's the way it is. If
you're looking for the comfort of not making mistakes
and not failing, you'll finish up mediocre . . . But
reaching greatness requires falling off the edge a load
of times and having the courage to get back up and get
on with it.*

Padraig Harrington

Mistakes are part of life and certainly part of the game of golf. For many people, however, they cannot accept mistakes because they feel embarrassed or ashamed about not doing something perfectly. These emotions arise because they are tied to their expectations as people and as golfers. In their minds, they believe that mistakes mean they have failed and fundamentally they are failures. Rather than recognising mistakes as information we can use to improve what we do, they see mistakes as information that confirms their view of themselves as failures.

This view of mistakes is unhelpful and damaging in sport because if we cannot allow ourselves to makes mistakes we are giving ourselves no opportunity to learn. We are not giving ourselves a chance to accept ourselves as humans and therefore fallible beings. We must be willing to fail in order to succeed. Imagine you are on the 18th green with a chance to win the competition you are playing by holing a par putt. The best way to stroke this putt with confidence and freedom is to feel that you can accept yourself as you are whether the putt rolls by or drops into the cup. In other words, the outcome of that putt does not change who you are or your value as a person.

Once we learn to separate our achievements from the value we place upon ourselves as people, we can begin to play with freedom. And we can learn from our mistakes, and move on from them, to continue playing golf as it should be played. The emotion tied to a mistake such as shame or guilt is replaced with a healthy emotion such as disappointment. We might be disappointed with the shot; however, we can accept it and learn from it. We begin to look forward to the next shot and dealing only with the demands of that shot.

Mistakes are necessary to play better golf. If we don't know what we did wrong, it's difficult to put it right. Change your view on mistakes – see them as a chance to learn and be willing to fail in order to succeed.

Fault 34: I never stick to my game plan during the game

How Common
is the Fault

How Difficult
to Fix

 I probably should have just run up there and hit because the more I backed off the more my arm started to shake and my hands were shaking. I'm all about speed, and I have a picture in my head of how hard I want to hit it and I just couldn't see that speed for some reason. I was just thinking about don't hit it fat, don't rip it by, don't do all this stuff, all these negative thoughts, so I backed away. Then I kind of heard something kind of rustling around and I backed away again. I was just trying to be as ready as I could be.

Jay Hass

Starting your game of golf without a plan is a sure way of performing less well than you ought to because, without a game plan, you might be taking unnecessary risks when you should be cautious - and cautious when you could take a reasonable risk. When we examine our scorecard, and the course, we can see what we are capable of, and what we expect of ourselves, in a reasonable manner. One way to gain confidence in our game is to allow ourselves to play to our strengths and we know our strengths before the game.

A sensible plan for most golfers is to assess their strengths and weaknesses against the course they intend to play. You should do this planning the evening, or morning, before you play your round of golf taking the course and weather conditions into consideration. The reasons you should do this planning before you play your round is to remove the emotion you are likely to feel during the round of golf. For example, if you are feeling ashamed because you missed a par putt on the par five 5th hole, you might want to get the dropped shot back on the

The Successful Golfer

par four 6th hole and pull out your driver; however, the landing area does not play to your strengths as a golfer. Your strength on this 6th hole might be two conservative iron shots to offer you a chance for a birdie. The lure of a wedge in your hand for the second shot to give you a chance for birdie becomes an emotional choice with a much lower percentage for a successful outcome overall. The conservative plan on this hole is the best choice.

You will perform best by assessing each hole in light of the current conditions and your strengths as a golfer. Our discipline for this game is up to ourselves. We must, where possible, remain confident in our game plan and act accordingly. We cannot go chasing after missed putts or poor bunker shots. Those parts of the game are over and we can only focus on what we do in the present.

Plan your game as best you can before you play. Aim to see each hole as separate from the hole you just played and the hole you are about to play.

Fault 35: Short putts are my Achilles heel

How Common
is the Fault

How Difficult
to Fix

> *Putting is the key to my mental game. It is a lot easier*
> *to accept hitting bad shots if you know you are putting*
> *well because you feel you can get the ball up and down*
> *and you can keep a score going. I find my patience*
> *runs out when I miss putts.*

Justin Rose

Most people expect short putts to be scored because the ball is resting three or four feet rather than 10 feet from the hole. For the uninitiated, it resembles a soccer ball just out from the goal line waiting for someone to tap it into the net. But for those who have played the game, their experience tells them something else – short putts easily slip by the hole. Those who play golf are aware that the wind, slope of the green, and stroke of the putter head all influence the outcome of a short putt. Perhaps the most troubling part of the process is what's going on inside the golfer's mind.

Although there is an expectation within, and outside, golf that short putts ought to be scored, this expectation differs among golfers. For some, the expectation is a challenge to organise oneself to putt positively while for others it is a threat not to leave it short or let it slip by the hole. The same putt, therefore, means different things to different golfers. It just depends on how you see it. A golfer that is confident about her putting will be less troubled by thoughts and feelings that she will miss this short putt, whereas a golfer that lacks confidence in her short putts will be more troubled by thoughts and feelings that she will miss this short putt.

There are at least two ways to solve this dilemma. In the long term, a golfer should practice short putts under stressful conditions. One way to do this is to set a target. For example, 15 three-foot putts in a row and if you miss one putt before you achieve your target - you must go back to the beginning and start again. As

81

you improve, your target will rise to 40, 60 or even 100 three-foot putts in a row. When you have practised deliberately in this way, you will have gained confidence and competence to putt well under pressure. A second strategy in the short term would be to pay attention to your breathing. Breathe in for four seconds and breathe out for eight seconds, allow the muscles in your shoulders and arms to relax, then approach the ball. At this stage, your hands and arms should feel soft. Now you can grip the club lightly and smoothly stroke the ball. This is a useful strategy because it helps us to focus upon something that will help us putt well and it helps to remove the jerky putting strokes golfers tend to make when they are anxious.

Practise short putts under stressful conditions. Give yourself the time to breathe in for 4 seconds and breathe out for 8 seconds before you stroke each putt, holding the putter lightly in your hands.

Fault 36: I can't stop thinking about the score during the game

How Common
is the Fault

How Difficult
to Fix

 I said to myself that nothing really spectacular had happened yet. I could chip this in or at least get it up and down. The best thing about that hole was where I got myself to in my head standing over the chip. Standing over it my mind was as clear as if I'd hit my two very best shots to be sitting there.

Padraig Harrington
who kept his focus to win his first major

The score matters to most golfers because it is an indication of how well, or poorly, they are playing compared with their usual scores, and those they are competing alongside. There is little point in denying the value of the score, especially if we are trying to suppress what it means to us. We must first acknowledge the score and what it means to us. We should make this acknowledgement as honestly as we can whilst being aware of how tightly or loosely we might bind it to our value as a golfer and as a person.

If the score is bound to your value of yourself as a worthy person, then it will be difficult for you to accept scores that do not reflect well upon you. You will need to learn to accept yourself as you are - rather than by the number you write on your scorecard. This is challenging for most people because they gain their value of themselves by comparing themselves with others. If you compare well to others, then you will feel good about yourself; however, if you compare poorly to others, then you will feel bad about yourself.

If we can accept the score on our scorecards without impinging on our value as people, we can begin to excel in golf. If you are a golfer who is happy when you play well and unhappy when you play poorly, then you might want to think about this situation for yourself. Being disappointed after a poor round of golf is normal. Feeling disgusted, shameful and guilty, however, is unfair on you especially if these feelings persist and are a regular part of your golfing life. When we are disappointed with our performance, we know that we can play well and we intend to do so the next day, following some specific practice or guidance from a teaching professional. When we feel ashamed of ourselves, we tend to hide away from doing what is helpful.

We recommend that you make a record of all your qualities as a person (e.g., I am happy, I am hard-working, I am honest, I am trustworthy) and keep this record where you can see it each day. These qualities underscore your worth as a person. These are your fundamental qualities. Your score in a game of golf might be important to you; however, it is not all that you are as a person. We ask golfers to record three personal qualities each day. The goal of this task is to broaden the list of qualities of each golfer as a *person* and build a stronger self-image. The same task can be used to build one's self-image as a golfer (I am honest, I am hard-working, I am focused, I trust my swing). When golfers recognise they are valuable people and golf is something that they do, it helps them to separate their scores on a scorecard from the value they place upon themselves as people.

Remember that you are a valuable, worthy person who plays golf. You are not a valuable and worthy person simply because you play golf well.

Fault 37: I can't stop worrying about what other people think of my golf

How Common
is the Fault

How Difficult
to Fix

> **"** *It's the screensaver on my laptop. I love that view down the hill on 10. It's my favourite spot at Augusta.* **"**
>
> **Rory McIlroy**
> responding to the question about his memory of the meltdown on the 10th hole at Augusta in April 2011

Other people will always think what they want to think – there is no relief from it. If we can accept that fact, then we save ourselves much angst and worry. What is the worst thing they can think about you as a golfer? You are not a good bunker player, you can't drive well off the first tee, you can't play well out of the rough and so on? It doesn't really matter what people think, that is their choice. We can only control what *we* think and what *we* feel about ourselves.

If we have grown up basing our value on others' opinions about us, we have yet to gain a fair and consistent view of ourselves. Imagine your self-esteem resembles a polystyrene cup filled with water. The cup fills up each time someone says something you would like to hear about yourself. But because you are easily hurt by others' harsh comments, your polystyrene cup develops little holes. You need more good comments to fill up your self-esteem but the holes in your cup keep draining you of your self-esteem. *The only way to keep your self-esteem filled up is by fixing the holes in the cup.* This will require you to depend less on others to ascertain your value of yourself. Choose to think about things you are (e.g., kind, caring, supportive) rather than things you achieve (e.g., winning at golf). Focusing on things you might achieve gives us little control about what happens to us.

Others think what they want because it's their choice. It also means you have the choice to think what you will - about yourself. Choose to value yourself with a yardstick that you control.

Fault 38: I can't cope with a negative playing partner

How Common
is the Fault

How Difficult
to Fix

> *Ronan is very clued in.*
> *After the second bad shot on the 18th [The Open*
> *Championship at Carnoustie, 2007] I was devastated.*
> *I had the feeling of being embarrassed. The feeling of*
> *embarrassment is worse than failure and it was*
> *starting to overwhelm me. I was quickly going to spiral*
> *downhill and Ronan did his job of convincing me of*
> *what I needed to do: 'Let's play one shot at a time,*
> *don't start getting into what it all means, we'll do the*
> *reflection afterwards'. It was all one-way talk going*
> *down that fairway. By the time I got to play my next*
> *shot I was right in the zone again. That's all down to*
> *him - no question. The interesting thing is he told me*
> *afterwards that he was thinking the same thing I was*
> *thinking, but he didn't let on. In his head he was*
> *thinking, 'I can't believe we've just lost The Open'.*
> *But he stuck to his guns*

Padraig Harrington

We play golf with all sorts of playing partners. Those who don't talk, those who don't stop talking, those who moan all the time and those who don't, those who think they are great at golf and those who don't. These are a selection of the personalities we encounter when we play golf and if we want to play golf competitively, we need to learn to play with them without their actions affecting how we play.

If you are aware of what you say, how you say it, and what you do on the golf

87

course, you'll easily recognise how positively or negatively those around you talk and behave. If you have learned to stay positive and learned to see golf as a challenge, you'll be surprised how two golfers can see the same situation differently. For instance, you and your partner hit your approach shots to the green but each ball slips into the greenside bunker. You, being a positive person, recognise that you would prefer your ball to have remained on the putting surface but you can see the challenge of getting up and down from where the ball has landed. Your partner, adopting a negative perspective, only recognises the lost opportunity of the ball not staying on the green. He starts to get annoyed with himself and lets all those around him know how annoyed he is. Knowing your partner, you realise that this attitude does not suit him as well as it suits others.

The lesson here is to continue to see a challenge in every situation you encounter on the golf course. Rather than being dragged down by your partner's negativity, you can choose to ask yourself: What is my challenge here? Only take responsibility for your thoughts, feelings and actions – not your partners. You do not need to change what your partners' think, feel and do, just lead by your good example.

We can only take responsibility for ourselves on the golf course. See the challenge in every situation, regardless of what others see. Relish the challenge!

Fault 39: I can't cope with distractions on the golf course

How Common
is the Fault

How Difficult
to Fix

 I was in my own little world, focusing on every shot. I wasn't thinking of what score I was or anything... But today was probably as good as I have ever played.

Darren Clarke
after he shot a record-equalling round of 60 in the
1999 European Open championship in Kildare, Ireland

Distractions are everywhere in golf. They can be visual (e.g., mud on the ball), auditory (e.g., the click of a camera) or from inside our heads (e.g., worrying about a water hazard). It is necessary, first, to establish which types of distractions affect you most when playing golf. Once you have established which distractions affect you most, you can begin to understand and address them. You might find that distractions only upset you sometimes, and at other times you are focused intensely on what you are doing regardless of what is happening around you.

One good example of how well we can concentrate is when we are at a driving range or short-game practice area. Often, there are people talking, eating, children laughing or shouting, and yet you continue to practise and practise well. So, what exactly is going on when you get distracted in golf? It's most likely that we shine our mental spotlight (i.e., the task on which we wish to concentrate) on the wrong cue. For example, it's natural to pay attention to a loud noise we hear, or notice how wet our grips have become on our clubs while playing in the rain. We might start thinking ahead about how we want to recover from a bogey on the previous hole. Once we are aware of these distractions, we can acknowledge and address them.

The Successful Golfer

We recommend using a pre-shot routine to focus on one thought at a time. You can learn to play each shot as if it was the only shot that matters. When you are practising, however, you can build in distractions to your practice so that you inoculate yourself for the games that matter most to you. For instance, you might play loud music while you putt. Or put some mud on the ball and try to hit the shot as if the mud were not there. You might practise hitting chip shots with grips and gloves that are dripping wet or ask a friend to distract you by playing slowly or rattling his clubs as you prepare to take your shot.

Coping with distraction is a skill we can learn. The more we practise with these distractions, the better we will cope with them when we encounter them on the golf course.

Fault 40: I am afraid I am going to make mistakes during the game

How Common is the Fault		
How Difficult to Fix		

 I stood over the ball, lining up the putt and suddenly I was gripped by negative thoughts. I couldn't visualize the ball going in. I was frightened of failure and I could barely draw back the putter to make contact with the ball.

Peter Alliss

Thinking that you are going to make mistakes during a game of golf sets you off down a road that ensures they will happen. But before we discuss such a circumstance, it's necessary to remember that mistakes are part of the game and the best golfers in the world make mistakes; however, they make fewer than most other golfers and when they do make a mistake, they recover quickly. It's realistic to expect that you will make some mistakes but we should not be worried about these mistakes. Instead, we should view golf as a challenge and our challenge is to practise and improve.

Everyone has a fear of failure to some extent and because of this fear of failing, we either work Spartan-like to avoid failure, or we let failure dominate our thoughts and actions. But letting failure dominate our thoughts and actions is not fair on ourselves because our minds are our allies and our minds want to work with us rather than against us. However, we must take charge. By taking charge of our minds, we work to discipline our thoughts. We recognize what can go wrong but we remain focused on thinking what we can control and what is within our ability to achieve.

When we think too far ahead, it is easy to worry about what might go wrong. Unfortunately, this way of thinking increases our worry and for most golfers, worry does not help them to play better.

Some golfers worry about their upcoming performance but they can cope with this worry because they have a strong sense of personal control in the competition. This sense of personal control might come from confidence to meet the challenges they face, or they might have simulated practice sessions as a dress rehearsal for the competition. They might have practised their pre-shot routine to help them focus on taking one shot at a time.

We need to acknowledge that mistakes are part of the game. And those mistakes do not mean you are a bad person or a bad golfer. They challenge us to improve, to focus on the shot at hand as if it were the only shot that matters. You'll feel much more relaxed about your game when you acknowledge that mistakes are part of the game.

Gene Sarazen said that he expected to hit six or eight poor shots, per round, which helped to relieve the pressure that he put on himself. This is a wise strategy and one you can adopt as a player. If you acknowledge before you begin your round that you are likely to hit ten poor shots, you can accept these poor shots when they happen. You can learn as best you can from these poor shots to reduce the number of poor shots you make as you improve.

Mistakes are part of golf; learn to accept them. Spend your time thinking about how you will react to mistakes because that is what matters most. Imagine yourself reacting confidently to the mistake, let the mistake go, and move on to your next shot.

Fault 41: I feel frustrated when I don't play to my expectations

How Common is the Fault		How Difficult to Fix	

Harrington has always seemed calm and controlled but, in reality, he was not. At least he was not until he made a conscious effort midway through last season to "mellow out".

"It had been that after a 72, I would walk off the golf course and be burning inside," he said. "I was stressed out. Something I had never had in the past. Before, I had a happy-go-lucky attitude. I would walk off the course after a 72 and think myself a bad person. "It has come from a need for me to grow, to separate things. If I hit a good shot, it doesn't make me a good person; if I hit a bad shot, it doesn't make me a bad person. I have to remember that I can't get too emotionally involved with the results. I like to say, 'I may be able to play golf but I don't get two votes in an election.'

Padraig Harrington

Our expectations, especially when they do not reflect our current abilities, can often lead to frustration. You might need to question whose expectations you are trying to meet. Are these expectations yours or someone else's? Do these expectations reflect how you are practising and performing right now?

Our expectations can work for, or against, us depending on how we set them up. What this means is that we need to be realistic but not too demanding so that we are challenged by what we do - but not fearful of every action we make.

Many golfers explain to us that they are doing all the right things – eating the right foods, working well at the gym, and spending time practising – but they cannot transfer it to the course. All these parts are necessary to play golf well and they matter to different degrees amongst different golfers. From a psychological perspective, however, we are especially interested in the practice structure for golfers. We tend to find that golfers are practising within a 'comfort zone' on the range rather than on the specific contours of the golf course. For instance, much time is spent hitting iron shots on the range but less so from downhill lies to a tight pin. Much less time is spent on the awkward stances in the bunker that ruin a scorecard on the 17th hole. Much less time is spent dealing with the thoughts and feelings of a 15-minute wait on the 16th tee when the golfer is leading the tournament.

The expectations golfers ought to have of themselves are best realised when practise becomes the hard part and playing becomes the easy part of golf. In other words, golfers ought to expect of themselves only what is typically achieved in practise under challenging conditions. It is important to remember that even with focused, diligent practice, success is never guaranteed and we ought to keep the game of golf in perspective. After the heartbreak of losing at the 1996 Masters, Greg Norman entered the interview room and laughed as he had all week. He explained: "It was all my mistakes today. I just didn't do the right things. I let it slip and I paid the price. It's not the end of the world. I'll wake up tomorrow and still be breathing."

 Start to base your expectations for competitive golf on your practice sessions but make an allowance for the thoughts and feelings you are likely to experience in competitive golf, especially the influence on you of those around you (i.e., other golfers and the audience).

Fault 42: I feel frustrated when I do not chip well

How Common
is the Fault

How Difficult
to Fix

 The usual scoring clubs for me - from 100 yards and in - have not been good enough. It has been a little bit that way the last few tournaments but it is something that never really worries me because I know they are my strengths.

Luke Donald

Good performance around the green is vital to playing golf well, whether it is getting the ball to roll close to the hole from a shot out of the bunker, pitching, or chipping the ball close to the hole and rolling in the putt. The more shots a golfer loses around the green, the more disheartening the game becomes because something is preventing the golfer from doing what he normally does well. We feel frustrated because we are prevented from doing what we intended to do.

Without a tolerance for frustration, we find it challenging to deal with things that do not go our way because we often hold an expectation that 'this misfortune should not happen to me' or 'it's unfair that I do not play as I know I can'. When Gary Player encountered the brutal pot bunkers at the 1955 Open Championship at St. Andrews, he said to his caddie: "…this isn't fair," to which his caddie replied, "…laddie, golf ain't meant to be fair."

If we can learn to tolerate more frustration (i.e., things not going the way we want them to go), we can deal better when these issues arise in future. This is known as high frustration tolerance – accepting the reality of frustration while keeping its awfulness in perspective. An example of this, on the golf course, would be when we hit a good drive that bounces into the rough on the last bounce. With a high frustration tolerance, a golfer can acknowledge that he does not like that this happened; however, he can accept it. It is fair to feel annoyed and disappointed without exaggerating these emotions into anger and self-pity.

In these situations, it is how we think that matters most. Instead of saying "I can't stand it when people don't act as they should on the golf course", we can think: "I don't like it but I can survive it and I don't need to get angry about it." For some golfers, the frustration of not playing well pushes them away from playing golf. Instead of: "I can't stand being frustrated around the greens, I'm going to avoid it from now on," the golfer can recognise that if he tries to avoid all frustration in golf, he wouldn't be playing golf at all: "Though I don't like being frustrated on the greens, I can tolerate it."

To build your tolerance for frustration, commit yourself to face at least some frustration on the golf course by telling yourself: "I don't like it but I can tolerate it" or challenging yourself to smile and accept the outcome of the shot when it didn't go as you intended it to.

Challenge yourself to tolerate those things you find frustrating while you play golf. Tell yourself that although you do not like what has happened - you can tolerate it.

Fault 43: I can't enjoy my round of golf

How Common
is the Fault

How Difficult
to Fix

 *I think Lee Trevino is the toughest I played against. He
loved to beat me but I loved playing him because I
knew he was going to be tough. I loved having great
competition. The stronger the competition,
the more fun it was.*

Jack Nicklaus

Golf is a sport and by its very nature, people play it because they enjoy it. And
things we enjoy doing, we tend to do well - whether it is work, music, or sport.
But what exactly do we enjoy about golf? This depends on the person and the
person's situation. For instance, most people enjoy being with their friends for a
round of golf, being congratulated for playing golf well, improving their skill set,
and winning tournaments.

Fundamentally, however, when we can do what is required of us on the golf
course, we enjoy the game most. The crucial part of the last sentence is "what is
required of us" which depends mostly on ourselves. For example, most touring
professionals would expect to get up and down from a greenside bunker that has a
50% difficulty rating for them. A low handicap golfer might expect to do the
same but might recognise that more practice and instruction is necessary to raise
their competence in this aspect of the game. A high handicap golfer ought to be
aware that getting up and down is much more challenging at this stage but with
practice and instruction can improve this element of the game.

For different reasons such as weather conditions, distractions, personal thoughts
and feelings, a golfer may not always play as well as she thinks she should. The
touring professional might shoot 6 over par; the low handicap golfer might have a
poor day with his driver, and the high handicap golfer might lose many more
shots around the green than usual. The difficulty arises when the golfer begins to

criticise rather than analyse mistakes. You would not choose to work with a teaching professional that criticises you, someone who provides no useful instruction or reward for your efforts. Yet we often treat *ourselves* in this harsh manner. It is best if we figure out rationally what ought to be improved and then work on that aspect of our game at the next practice session. Learn to reward and encourage yourself three times more than you criticise yourself.

When we treat ourselves with respect, we feel more able to do what we are doing well. Aim to encourage yourself during practice and competition as a good coach would.

Fault 44: I can't stop doubting myself on the course

How Common
is the Fault

How Difficult
to Fix

 You know the biggest and most important thing in
playing a golf shot is committing 100 per cent to your
decision. Commitment in terms of the stroke, your
emotion and your feel. Sometimes that level of
commitment needs verbal affirmation. It is what gives
you the bottle to ignore the little voice saying: 'This
can go wrong and that can go wrong'.

Nick Faldo

Most golfers believe certain things about themselves: "I'm a good ball striker" or
"I can't cope with short putts". When they look in the mirror they see a certain
reflection that either represents a confident image of a golfer, or a sliding scale of
confidence to a player who cannot commit to accepting himself or herself as an
able golfer. What's most interesting about this image in the mirror is that it is just
someone's perception of the image. They make inferences about the golfer and
believe things that often have no evidence to support any claim. Or if they do
have evidence, it is skewed and filtered to such a degree that only those pieces of
evidence that fit the golfer's image are accepted and internalised.

Some doubt is helpful because it prompts us to take action. It prompts us to care
about what we are doing and work hard at our game. But when such doubt turns
to fear, we become restricted in everything we do on the course. We become less
than we are capable. This doubtful and fearful state changes what we think, feel
and do as well as the physiological reactions within our body.

We have at least two ways to dispute this fear. First, we can ask ourselves in
positive terms: 'What's my challenge on this shot?' Once we have identified the
challenge we can choose the shot that we feel most comfortable executing. If we
are fearful about using a three-wood to reach a green, we might choose a seven-

iron and a wedge. If we are fearful about chipping over a bunker to a tight pin, we can usually choose an alternative route. You might argue that such strategies are avoiding the real challenge; however, we are aiming to move from doubt and fear to control and confidence. We are finding a way back to a place that strengthens our self-image as a golfer. Through more focused practice, we can begin to choose our three-wood or our chip to a tight pin.

The second strategy builds on the first. Step out of your doubtful world into the cocoon of your pre-shot routine. A cocoon that helps you to let go of all expectations – see the target and let the ball go to the target.

We can choose what we think about ourselves. But to choose properly, we must spend time thinking good things about ourselves. We need to tell ourselves what we are capable of achieving and commit to execute each shot with confidence.

Fault 45: I can't manage my anger after a bad shot

How Common
is the Fault

How Difficult
to Fix

 That's the first good shot I've played all day.

Seve Ballesteros
speaking to his friend Antonio Carriles on hitting a
ball to within 1 foot of the pin after hitting the
preceding 120 balls to within ten feet of the pin.

The first question to ask is what makes you angry? Is it just hitting a bad shot or is it what the bad shot makes you feel about yourself? We all hit bad shots and we all react differently to those bad shots, but it is how we deal with that reaction that determines how we continue to play afterwards. Some golfers get angry with themselves and they can control their anger to benefit their games. But for many golfers, anger is one emotion that interferes strongly with their performance.

When we examine our anger, we can rationalize what is happening to us and deal effectively with that anger. Becoming a more accepting golfer that accepts the outcome of each shot, regardless of whether it is what the golfer expected or not, is what will give us the greatest enjoyment in the game.

Take most pride in the process you have developed for hitting each shot – let other people make what they will from the outcome. This is not an easy part of one's game to change. After all, most golfers have spent their lives looking at where their golf ball finishes and then judging themselves. It would be much better not to judge yourself at all. It does not mean that you do not care about the outcome of each shot; it just means you have accepted the outcome before it happens whether the ball rolls into the hole or off the green.

When you accept the outcome of a shot before it happens, you will have gained a freedom few others enjoy. In golf and other sports, it is the key to success. You are doing all that you can to allow the ball to go to your target but you have already accepted the outcome. We know you are doing all you can because you have chosen a target, used a pre-shot routine, and committed to the shot. As soon as the ball leaves the putter or clubface, you are just watching it to find out where it lands – nothing more.

If your anger is hurting your golf performance you need to give yourself a break from the expectations that you set for yourself. By lowering the bar and accepting the outcome of each shot, we can become more emotionally controlled and get back to playing our best golf.

Fault 46: When I lose my confidence I can't seem to get it back

How Common
is the Fault

How Difficult
to Fix

    The bogeys on 6 and 7 just killed me. I just couldn't
pick myself up and felt the life drain out of me.
Everything I tried just went wrong.

Graeme McDowell

Every golfer loses confidence at one stage of his or her career. For some golfers, they lose confidence for a short period of time but for others the loss of confidence can be much longer and last for several years. The latter occurrence is an unfortunate circumstance because this loss of confidence, or slump, is reversible – the golfer just needs to get the mental game back on track.

Losing one's confidence is most often associated with less effort and enthusiasm for practice as well as not paying attention to the fundamentals of the game. And this adds to the downward spiral of one's game. When a golfer loses confidence, it is best to review the segments of his or her golf game and see what needs adjustment - not necessarily complete changes. In some instances, it might simply be best to allow yourself to reduce the demands on yourself in practice and competition.

Because confidence in golf encapsulates skills such as driving, iron play, pitching and putting, it's likely that a golfer will rate her confidence differently on these different skills. This is the first step in the process to regaining lost confidence. Once you have honestly rated your confidence for each element of the game, you can rate the skill that is most important to you and begin with a diet of success on this skill. In putting, for example, you might stroke the ball into the cup ten times from one foot before moving the ball to 2 feet, then 3 feet, and so on. Next, you can reinforce yourself positively by encouraging effort and attention to your routine, and accepting the outcome of each shot. Then, you can create more elaborate practice plans that build your skills in the game. For example, you might choose to hit 10 consecutive 60-yard pitch shots to within 20 feet of the pin. As you gain competence and confidence at this skill, you might aim to hit 10 consecutive 60-yard pitch shots to within 15 feet of the pin and so on. The aim here is to choose a challenging goal that has a specific target which you can measure but which is within your capabilities at that time.

Confidence is a belief in your ability to complete a task. Build your confidence with a diet of success and begin to act as if you are already a confident golfer.

Fault 47: I have a great fear of three putting

How Common
is the Fault

How Difficult
to Fix

 *You know, bad times in golf are more frequent than the
good times. I've always been pretty hard on myself
when I fail because I don't find it very easy to accept
that. And there's times I've been completely and
utterly fed up with the game. But friends and family
say, get out there and practise and keep going, keep
going, keep going, and that's why I'm sitting here now.*

Darren Clarke
after winning the 2011 British Open at Sandwich

We are intrigued by the number of times that golfers talk about fear on the golf
course. Here are some of the most common fears: three-putting, hitting the ball
out of bounds, water hazards, first tee shots, and looking foolish and incompetent.

If we consider that many of the instructions we hear in life and sport begin with
"Don't....", we can understand that our focus is on what to avoid rather than what
we ought to do. "Don't be naughty"; "Don't put your feet on the seat"; "Don't hit
it left off the tee"; "Don't leave it short" and so on. If we simply restated these
instructions in positive terms we might say: "Be good"; "Keep your feet on the
floor"; "Aim down the right side of the fairway"; and "Stroke it to the hole".

Many of the golfers we support are encouraged to do things in positive terms. If a
golfer is worried about three putting, he can think of a positive instruction for
himself: "Follow my routine and stroke it to the hole". If a golfer has a tight lie
and has a pitch to the green, he chooses a positive instruction: "What's my target
here? I'll focus my gaze completely on that landing area." Or they might focus
upon general positive instructions as they play a round of golf: "I'll encourage
myself before and after every shot I take today." These are relatively easy things

to say; doing them, however, is more challenging!

Doing them consistently is the most challenging part of all and it is why we encourage golfers to *persist* in being a good coach to themselves.

Be a good coach to yourself. Give yourself positive instructions to follow and say nice things to yourself as often as you can.

Fault 48: I can't maintain my tempo late in the round

How Common is the Fault

How Difficult to Fix

 He never looked like he rushed it; never looked like he ever tried to hit one hard. He had one smooth, slow tempo.

Wild Bill Mehlhorn
talking about Harry Vardon

The view a golfer takes of the final holes in a round of golf often determines the outcome of the game. And if that view is so crucial to the outcome of the game, then recognizing your tempo, and maintaining a focus on the tempo that serves you best, is time well spent.

One reason our tempo changes is because we think about things in the past or things in the future that interfere with our focus right now. During the final holes of a round of golf, we might be considering that a birdie on the next hole will be our best round of golf, or that it will win the tournament. Unfortunately, when we think about these outcomes, we cause ourselves to become more anxious and excited than we need to be, and our expectations interfere with our tempo.

With regard to swing tempo, research suggests that anxious feelings sometimes feel uncomfortable for us and one way to overcome this uncomfortable feeling is to get on with the action quickly. Many people feel anxious in the dentist's waiting room before going for a filling because they have no sense of personal control in this situation. Their fears are allayed somewhat when the dentist explains what she is going to do, and what to expect. In golf, we can recognise how we are feeling and accept that these feelings are normal and helpful. We can learn to relax by breathing deeply and allowing our shoulders, arms and hands to feel soft. Then we begin our routine as normal, paying attention to the target and allowing ourselves to athletically stroke the ball to the target. To recognize our tempo while practising, it is a good idea to work backwards from your fastest swing, slowing down your swing to a pace that you find comfortable and one that provides the best ball strike that you are capable of doing. Try to recreate that tempo in a practice swing before you strike the ball. If you tend to strike faster when the ball is in front of you, slow down your practice swing to encourage yourself to swing within yourself - until you are swinging as evenly and naturally as possible. On the course, you can repeat this swing tempo before you strike your shot.

Our emotions cause us to behave in ways that reflect our natural tendency to fight, flee, or freeze. When we get anxious we swing faster than usual. Discipline yourself to make a practice swing that is slower and more composed than normal. This practice will encourage you to swing within yourself.

Fault 49: I can't trust my swing after a poor tee shot

How Common
is the Fault

How Difficult
to Fix

*I arrived at Lytham [in 1969] feeling confident and
ready to win. I'd won in America the year before and
knew I had the capability. I'd worked hard on my
tempo, concentrating on my legs and lower body so
that I could control the speed of my swing at will.
Under pressure, and with the adrenalin rush, I had a
tendency to get quicker. I had to learn to control that
to become a consistent winner. I hit thousands of balls
and had it perfected when I got there.*

Tony Jacklin

If we accept that we make mistakes in golf, then any poor tee shot is just one shot
that has gone wrong. The last shot you hit or the next shot you hit has no bearing
on this shot. Remember that it is only you who knows whether you have hit a
poor tee shot.

Trust is built up by working hard on your swing but also by being athletic and
agreeing with yourself that what you have done is correct and reflects the hard
work you have put in. Trust is self-belief in yourself and your skills. Trust is the
positive things you say to yourself every time you practise and play. Allow
yourself to accept the poor tee shot and prepare for the next shot.

But why is it so hard to let go of the memory of a poor tee shot? There are several
ways to explain this phenomenon. First, you might have recent experiences in
which you hit a poor tee shot and subsequent shots were also poor, reinforcing
your belief that poor shots follow a poor tee shot. Second, the emotion attached to
a poor tee shot might be an unhealthy emotion. For instance, you might feel
shame after a poor tee shot rather than disappointment or you might feel anxious
about an upcoming shot rather than concern. You might argue that there is little

difference between these emotions; however, they have a profound effect on how we think and act after experiencing unhealthy and healthy emotions. For instance, when we feel shame, we might hide or withdraw from a similar action in the future whereas if we are disappointed, we might seek an opportunity to execute the shot again - as we know we are capable of striking the ball well.

We ought to allow ourselves to make mistakes to learn. We can analyse our mistakes but not criticise ourselves for making them. Some golfers give themselves five seconds to rehearse the correct swing, then put the club back into their bag and look forward to the challenge of the next shot.

One poor shot is no reflection of your ability as a golfer or the quality of your swing. Look forward to the challenge of the next shot and let your swing do its thing.

Fault 50: Slow players frustrate me and make me play poorly

How Common is the Fault		
How Difficult to Fix		

> **"** *Bernhard Langer was clean-shaven when we set off.*
> *Now he has a beard this long.* **"**

Lee Trevino
about the time taken by the group ahead of him

Slow play is part of golf. And being part of golf, we need to accept that it is part of the game; we need to learn to deal with it efficiently. It is a good idea to raise your level of frustration tolerance because it will serve you well in reaching your potential. Some professional golfers explain that pro-am tournaments can disrupt their preparation for a tournament because play slows down and they cannot deal effectively with slow play.

Slow play can occur in any tournament, not just in a pro-am. The challenge for most golfers is to have something useful to do with their time rather than thinking (or worrying) about the next shot. Many golfers undermine themselves during this time. For example, it's not uncommon for a player waiting on the 16th tee to hit his tee shot out of bounds after a 15 minute wait. Golfers, like Tiger Woods, refer to this 'waiting time' as 'cooling off'. Cooling off can sometimes occur when the practice area is a long distance from the 1st tee.

Most golfers might need to warm-up their swing again after a 15- or 20-minute wait. They can begin by swinging a club to feel loose and warm their muscles. They can place a tee in the ground as a target to aim at in the full swing - as suggested by the legendary teaching professional, Harvey Penick.

The behaviour of others, players or spectators, is none of your concern. When it's time to hit your shot, you enter the bubble of your routine and that will take care of your concerns for you.

Putting the Mental Game into Action

Perhaps the truest test of a player is whether you can rise to the greatest of occasions. When you are on the course you have to be able to concentrate at the right times and to think clearly at the right times. But it starts even before you get to an event: you have to be able to take your game with you and raise it up for the occasion.

Jack Nicklaus

Having read this book so far, you should have developed a sound understanding of what it takes for you to achieve your potential in golf. But like all golf skills, to improve, you need to practise your mental skills consistently.

From the beginning of this book you will have identified which golfer you are most like, the one from the Old Course or the one from the New Course. You might have some characteristics of the players from each course but the most important part of having read the player descriptions is that you *choose to do something* about what you have learned. We only improve when we make a commitment to improve. And we must work hard to remain committed to see that improvement through even when we feel like giving up.

In the next section, we offer the lessons learned from 30 research studies on golf. These studies have examined: how we should practise golf skills, what we should think about when we putt, and how the speed and movement of our golf swing is affected by stress. We are sure that the lessons that follow will help you become a successful golfer.

The Successful Golfer

Part 2

Research Bunker #1: Reflecting positively on performance improves motivation

The Study

Eighty novice golfers participated in a putting competition. After the competition, half of the participants were asked to reflect on what went well, while the others did a control task to occupy the mind (it was a simple concentration task). The golfers who were asked to reflect on what went well during the task showed better patterns of thinking, whether they won or lost the putting competition, than those who did the concentration task. This better pattern of thinking meant that the golfers explained their performance levels by referring to things they could personally control and so felt able to change their performance levels in the future.

Application

This study outlines the importance of identifying positive elements of your game following successful and unsuccessful competitions. By thinking of things that you have done well - you recognise that performance is a result of actions that you can control, which is helpful for enhancing motivation to practice.

Key Point

After a round of golf, recall three things that went well for you (e.g., a creative chip on the 13th hole). These three elements of your golf game reinforce feelings of personal control, which will drive your will to practise, improve your skills and lower your score.

Allen, M. S., Jones, M. V., & Sheffield, D. (2010). The influence of positive reflection on attributions, emotions, and self-efficacy. *The Sport Psychologist, 24,* 211-226.

Research Bunker #2: If you want to putt well don't think about it!

The Study

A group of novice golfers were given instructions from typical coaching guidelines about how to putt. They used these guidelines to practice putting. A separate group of novice golfers were asked to practice putting but they were not given any coaching guidelines. This second group were also prevented from forming any rules of thumb when putting by having to pay attention to a task requiring them to shout out a random letter on the beat of a metronome. Both groups were then asked to perform under stressful conditions. There was a decrease in the putting performance of the group who had learned using coaching instructions whereas the putting performance of the group who had not formed any rules of thumb about putting increased.

Application

These findings suggest that when golfers perform under pressure, their performances get worse because they revert to focussing on the rules they have for executing the putt – rather than just putting without thinking. This "paralysis by analysis" happens when golfers are placed under competitive pressure and in an effort to do well they consciously focus on making sure the movement is done correctly. For example, a golfer who concentrates on making sure the movement of his putting stroke is correct while trying to putt. Paradoxically concentrating on controlling a motor movement (like a putting stroke) usually leads to a worse putting performance because the movement becomes less fluid.

Key Point

Anything that occupies the mind to prevent a conscious control of the movement, such a trigger word (e.g., smooth) or phrase (e.g., back and through), can help when putting under pressure.

Masters, R.S.W. (1992). Knowledge, nerves and know-how: The role of explicit vs. implicit knowledge in the breakdown of a complex skill under pressure. *British Journal of Psychology, 83*, 343-358.

Research Bunker #3: Be careful what you think!

The Study

Undergraduates participated in a golf-putting task and began by taking some practice trials with no specific instructions. They then took two putts, and for one of the putts were told to land the ball on the target. For the other putt, they were told to land the ball on the target but to be particularly careful not to hit the ball past the target. Some of the participants did these putting tasks while being asked to keep a six-digit number in mind. The participants who were asked to keep this six digit number in mind were more likely to hit the ball past the target when told explicitly not to.

Application

Under normal circumstances we are able to avoid making mistakes because our mind unconsciously monitors threats to the things we wish to achieve. But when we have a lot on our mind (such as trying to remember a six digit number) our conscious minds are occupied and thoughts that we tried to suppress, such as overshooting the target, pop back into our head. This study showed that thoughts about what we do not want to happen may end up coming true – under conditions of high mental load. Obviously golfers do not try to putt while remembering a six digit number but another, more common, example of a high mental load is when we are anxious and our mind becomes preoccupied with worries and concerns. So under conditions of high anxiety we may end up doing exactly what we tried to avoid. When playing golf, keep a focus on what you wish to achieve, or reduce mental load by relaxation.

Key Point

When our mind is occupied, for example with worries or concerns, we may end up doing exactly what we tried to avoid.

Wegner, D. M., Ansfield, M., & Pilloff, D. (1998). The putt and the pendulum: Ironic effects of the mental control of action. *Psychological Science, 9,* 196-199.

Research Bunker #4: The psychological approach to golf does make a difference

The Study

Data were collected from golfers, with a range of handicaps, on their psychological approach to golf. Skilled golfers (i.e., lower handicap) reported greater concentration, commitment, better mental preparation and were more able to regain attention following distraction. Conversely, lower handicap golfers were less prone to negative emotions and negative thoughts.

Application

The psychological approach to golf does matter. So taking time to develop the right psychological approach and using techniques like imagery, self-talk, and relaxation techniques are worthwhile. It is a continuous process but just like all mental skills you can improve them with practice. Be patient because it takes time, just like learning any physical skill. To illustrate, the first time you consciously try to reduce your negative thoughts (then your total thoughts) during a round of golf may consist of 80% negative thoughts but if you consciously try to think of task relevant, positive, or even neutral thoughts then your negative thoughts during competition may only be 75% of your total thoughts - an improvement. Next competition you can aim to reduce your negative thoughts to 65% and so on. Keep progressing. It is a process that you can actively control – don't feel that your thoughts and what you say to yourself 'just happen' – you can work to control them.

Key Point

Skilled golfers have better psychological approaches to golf; however, these are approaches that can be developed by any player over time to improve performance.

Thomas, P. R., & Over, R. (1994). Psychological and psychomotor skills associated with performance in golf. *The Sport Psychologist, 8,* 73-86.

Research Bunker #5: Imagery and self-talk can help you play better

The Study

Amateur golfers attended five separate sessions in which they were trained to use mental imagery and self-talk. Mental imagery is like running movies in your mind and self-talk is saying things to yourself that help you play golf better. At the end of the training sessions the golfers said their psychological approach to competition had improved and perhaps more importantly their handicap decreased over the eight weeks in which the study was run.

Application

Psychological skills are important because they bring performance benefits and in this instance it was observed after only eight weeks of practise. Imagery can help you picture and feel what you want to do on the golf course and self-talk can be used for a range of useful functions, including maintaining focus, boosting confidence and thinking smartly in difficult situations. These outcomes are all helpful for improving performance on the golf course but remember these skills will only be useful to you if you practise them.

Key Point

Psychological skills can help improve your performance on the golf course in a matter of weeks so long as you practise these skills often.

Thomas, P. R., & Fogarty, G. J. (1997). Psychological skills training in golf: The role of individual differences in cognitive preferences. *The Sport Psychologist, 11,* 86-106.

Research Bunker #6: Top professionals think better

The Study

Fourteen top professional golfers and a comparison group of nine club professionals were interviewed about their psychological approach to golf. Top professionals were more focused during tournaments reflecting a special depth of concentration and were better able to cope with distractions compared with club professionals.

Application

The results from this study are stimulating because they illustrate that even within a group of talented golfers (tournament and teaching professionals) differences in psychological factors emerge. These differences again highlight the importance of having a psychological approach for playing golf because the best professionals had a better psychological approach than the teaching professionals.

Key Point

Even among professional golfers differences in psychological approach occur with the more successful golfers having a better psychological approach.

McCaffrey, N., & Orlick, T. (1989). Mental factors related to excellence among top professional golfers. *International Journal of Sport Psychology, 20,* 256-278.

Research Bunker #7: Where you focus your attention is important to play well

The Study

Nineteen professional and collegiate golfers were interviewed about the psychological characteristics of peak performance. In other words, what they were thinking about when they were playing really well. During peak performance, the golfers were highly focused and immersed in the task at hand. In general, a narrow focus of attention appeared ideal for peak performance but what golfers chose to focus on differed across players with some golfers preferring to focus internally (e.g., thoughts, feelings), while others preferred to focus externally (e.g. on a specific target).

Application

Being focused – paying attention to things that are helpful to performance – is an important factor in golf performance. In this sample of golfers, there were differences across golfers about what they paid attention to when they were playing well. Regardless of how you choose to focus your attention it is important to direct your attention to something so that your swing is not affected by distractions, such as negative thoughts about performance.

Key Point

There is no one style of attention that is suitable for all golfers – so finding out where your attention is focused when playing well and trying to maintain that as often as possible is key.

Cohn, P. J. (1991). An exploratory study on peak performance in golf. *The Sport Psychologist, 5,* 1-14.

Research Bunker #8: Sticking to a pre-shot routine will help you perform better

The Study

Three elite American collegiate golfers were encouraged to be consistent in the use of their pre-shot routine. The golfers initially showed more consistent use of their pre-shot routine and four months later, all three participants were recording fewer shots during rounds than before the intervention.

Application

A consistent pre-shot routine can help improve performance by focusing attention on the task at hand and occupying one's mind. Not only can elements of a pre-shot routine help performance in themselves (e.g., the use of imagery can increase the likelihood of a successful shot) but they can also be effective by occupying the mind and preventing unwanted distractions taking hold.

Key Point

Once you have a routine that is effective in helping you to stay relaxed and focused for each stroke then apply that routine consistently in both practice and competition.

Cohn, P. J., Rotella, R. J., & Lloyd, J. W. (1990). Effects of a cognitive-behavioural intervention on the preshot routine and performance in golf. *The Sport Psychologist, 4,* 33-47.

Research Bunker #9: On what should you concentrate to hit more accurate shots in golf?

The Study

Golfers are often unsure about what exactly they should pay attention to during the golf shot. The accumulating research encourages us to pay attention externally rather than internally. An external focus of attention means that the golfer pays attention to the motion of the club (something outside the golfer's body) whereas an internal focus of attention means that the golfer pays attention to the movement of their arms (something within the golfer's body). Gabriele Wulf and colleagues at the University of Nevada examined this idea between two groups of novice golfers practising pitch shots. The external focus group was instructed to focus on the pendulum-like motion of the golf club whereas the internal focus group focused on their arm movements. The external focus group were much more accurate in their pitch shots than the internal focus group.

Application

We perform better in golf when we pay attention to aspects of the golf game that do not interfere with executing golf skills. It seems sensible to find a focus outside your body (e.g., a pendulum motion, a spot on a golf ball) to hit shots more accurately.

Key Point

It seems that our minds cope best when attention is focused outside our bodies. Our minds cannot work well when we analyse actions we can execute without analysis.

Badami, R., VaezMousavi, M., Wulf, G., & Namazizadeh, M. (2011). Feedback after good versus poor trials affects intrinsic motivation. *Research Quarterly for Exercise and Sport, 2,* 360-365.

Research Bunker #10: Stress can affect the movement of your golf swing

The Study

Nine golfers were filmed striking their tee-shot from the 1st tee during three separate club competitions and their swings were compared with five practice shots taken with an identical club. The shots in competition were the high stress scenario and the five practice shots were the low stress scenario. Analysis of the swing parameters indicated the swings were different between low and high stress situations; however, the only clear pattern to emerge was an increase in swing tempo during the competition swings. The backswing times and the downswing phase were quicker in competition.

Application

Why golfers should swing quicker in competition than practice is unclear. But what can happen when placed under stress is players feel uncomfortable and, because of that feeling, they rush their shots to escape the feelings of discomfort. The use of techniques to maintain a consistent rhythm, when swinging in competition and practice may help – for example counting a beat on the backswing and the follow through (this technique may also be useful in stopping any anxious thoughts about the swing coming to the fore). Where possible a golfer should adopt the same relaxed tempo in competition as practice.

Key Point

Be aware that your swing tempo may change from practice to competition and so take steps to keep it consistent.

De Ste Croix, M. B. A., & Nute, M. (2008). The effects of cognitive anxiety on the biomechanical characteristics of the golf swing. *Biology of Sport, 25,* 3-11.

Research Bunker #11: Just let those worries out

The Study

Some people who report low anxiety show contrasting physiological and behavioural responses. In other words they say that they are not really anxious but the reactions in their bodies and how they behave do not seem to match. These people are said to repress their feelings of anxiety. Tim Woodman and Paul Davis asked some novice golfers to engage in a putting task. Those participants who repress anxiety (a mentally effortful task) were more likely to putt past a target when told explicitly 'not to' under conditions of stress. Under normal circumstances we are able to avoid making mistakes because our mind unconsciously monitors threats to what we wish to achieve. But when we have a lot on our mind (such as trying not to think about how anxious we feel) our conscious minds are occupied and those thoughts that we tried to suppress about what we did not want to happen (like putting past the target), pop back into our head. In this instance the golfers did the very thing they were told not to do.

Application

Thoughts about what we do not want to happen may end up coming true – if we are preoccupied with not feeling our anxiety. In short, acknowledge feeling nervous or anxious and recognise that they are a normal part of playing golf, or reduce the feeling with a relaxation technique.

Key Point

If you feel anxious, acknowledge it and accept it. Interpret you anxious thoughts and feelings as an indication that your body is preparing for competition.

Woodman, T., & Davis, P. A. (2008). The role of repression in the incidence of ironic errors. *The Sport Psychologist, 22,* 183-196.

Research Bunker #12: How quickly do golfers' performances decline as they get older?

The Study

At the 2009 British Open, at Turnberry, eight-time Major winner, Tom Watson, had a chance to become the oldest winner ever of the tournament. His approach shot to the green landed exactly where he wanted but momentum meant it crept over the edge of the green. He had to get up and down to win the tournament but unfortunately it wasn't to be on this occasion. He eventually lost in a play-off to Stewart Cink. One question that gained great media interest after Tom Watson's loss was whether he was too old to win the tournament? The research exploring whether cognitive (i.e., thinking) and physical performances decline as we age suggest that they do at a rate of 0.5% per year from the years of best performances; though a recent study on the performance of champion golfers suggests that the story might be different in golf. Joseph Baker and his colleagues at York University in Canada explored the performance careers of 17 professional golfers. The average rate of decline for golfers between the ages of 35 and 49 was only 0.07%. From ages 51-60, however, the average rate of decline grew to 0.26%.

Application

These results suggest that the rate of decline in skilled golf performance is much less than the declines seen from more generic research. Are these declines just a fact of getting older? This may not be the case and disparities could simply be due to differences in sports and levels of practice. For example, the training profiles of Master athletes show that the content and volume of their training is significantly less than that of younger athletes.

Key Point

While golfers' performances do decline with age the rate is much less in golf than for other sports.

Baker, J., Horton, S., Pearce, W., & Deakin, J. (2005). A longitudinal examination of performance in champion golfers. *High Ability Studies, 16,* 179-185.

Research Bunker #13: Understanding and preventing choking

The Study

Eleven elite golfers were interviewed about their ability to cope with pressure. The golfers were either professional, or had a single-figure handicap. Six of the golfers frequently choked in competition, while five regularly performed well under pressure. The information from the golfers was complemented by interviews with four experienced professional golf coaches who had all worked with golfers who had choked or performed well under pressure. Distraction was identified as the main reason for choking. Distraction can come from many sources, but in this sample it came primarily from internal thoughts such as worrying about past shots and being concerned about failure. Other major sources of choking identified were anxiety which is exacerbated by the golfers feeling unable to cope with, or control, their thoughts, feelings and performance. To help prevent choking, practical and psychological strategies were suggested. Practical techniques included having consistent and well-practiced pre- and post-shot routines, and practising under pressure. Psychological strategies included reframing negative thoughts (for example, recognising a difficult putt as a challenge) and using imagery to rehearse the shot before executing it.

Application

The data from the golfers and coaches are valuable because there were clear differences between the golfers who were able to cope with pressure and those that were not. This illustrates that choking, and performing poorly is not necessarily a certainty and is not always going to happen. By adopting, and practising practical and psychological strategies you are taking personal control which makes performing well under pressure more likely.

Key Point

Choking under pressure is not guaranteed and it is possible to reduce the likelihood of choking by using appropriate coping strategies.

Hill, D., Hanton, S., Matthews, N., & Fleming, S. (2010). A qualitative exploration of choking in elite golf. *Journal of Clinical Sport Psychology, 4,* 221 – 240

Research Bunker #14: Some friendly words can help with putting

The Study

Eighty sport science students at a British University completed a golf-putting task in which they were required to putt from ten feet on an artificial putting matt. Before commencing the putting task, which consisted of ten putts, the experimenters gave half the participants 'social-support instructions' which were designed to boost self-esteem (e.g., we are confident you will perform well), and emotional support (e.g., we will be here to help throughout the task). The participants who received the social support which consisted of these esteem-boosting instructions and emotional support performed better on the putting task. The effect was particularly strong for those participants who had been identified by the experimenters before the task as perceiving they had a low level of social support in general.

Application

What this study illustrates is that social support, in this instance through some well-chosen words, can help golf performance. It is particularly helpful if you perceive yourself to have a low level of social support in general. This type of social support may be effective because it relaxes the golfer and helps to create a more positive emotional state for performance. Of course, in golf there are clearly significant others such as coaches, and in particular caddies, who can play a role in providing social support, and ultimately help enhance performance.

Key Point

Social support from significant others can help you relax and enhance your performance.

Rees, T.J., & Freeman, P. (2010). Social support and performance in a golf-putting experiment. *The Sport Psychologist, 24,* 333-348.

Research Bunker #15: Skilled Golfers should focus on the flight of the ball and not on the swing movement

The Study

Many studies have shown that focussing attention internally and trying to consciously control the movements of a golf swing can result in impaired performance. There is a particular tendency for golfers to do this when under pressure. To explore where attention should be focussed, 33 golfers were asked to execute a chip shot from 20 metres towards a flag. The golfers were all skilled with an average handicap of 5.5 and the highest handicap was 9.4. One group of golfers was asked to focus on the motion of the arms during the swing and to repeat the phrase "wrist hinge" to help this focus. The second group was asked to focus on the position of the clubface through the swing and to repeat the phrase "square face" to help this focus. The final group of participants was asked to focus on the flight of the ball after it left the clubface and to repeat the phrase "straight flight" to help this focus. Chipping performance in both the normal and pressure conditions was best in the group asked to focus on the flight of the ball and was significantly higher than both other groups. The group who focused on the position of the clubface was, in turn, better than the group asked to focus on the motion of the arms.

Application

Choosing to focus attention externally, such as on the trajectory of the shot, can prevent attention being directed towards the movements of a shot. Golf shots are best executed without conscious focus on the movement.

Key Point

Once you are skilled at golf, one technique to make sure you perform well under pressure is to focus attention on external factors relevant to the shot, such as the flight of the ball, and not the movement of your body.

Source: Bell, J. J., & Hardy, J. (2009). The effect of attentional focus on golf performance. *Journal of Applied Sport Psychology, 21,* 163-177.

Research Bunker #16: Stick to a routine (That Works)

The Study

Pre-shot routines can be an effective way to enhance performance in golf. Six male golfers who had played representative golf for England were asked about their pre-shot routines. The composition of the routines outlined by the golfers included both behavioural and psychological elements. Examples of behavioural elements included the use of a practice swing, placing the ball and setting the stance. Examples of psychological elements included imagining the ball coming off the club face or seeing ball going in the hole. All participants mentioned the importance of sticking to the routine consistently, and would abort and re-start the routine if they did not feel ready; however, on occasions some golfers did report continuing to strike the ball even when they did not feel ready and this typically happened in tense situations.

Application

This study illustrates one way in which anxiety can affect performance by making a person 'hurry up' to remove themselves from the unpleasant anxiety-inducing situation. This can manifest itself in golfers 'rushing their shot' particularly the most important ones. In all settings, but particularly tense, important situations, it is important to stick to a consistent pre-shot routine to help relax, focus attention on the task at hand, and increase the likelihood of success.

Key Point

Sticking to a consistent pre-shot routine can be one way of ensuring that you do not 'rush' your shot - which can happen when placed under pressure.

Cotterill, S., Sanders, R., & Collins, D. (2010) Developing effective pre-performance routines in golf: Why don't we ask the golfer? *Journal of Applied Sport Psychology, 22,* 51-64.

Research Bunker #17: Practice to compete

The Study

A putting task required 32 novice golfers to putt at a target (a square of red tape) on an indoor putting green from nine different locations. The participants performed the task under both low and high stress before taking part in a training condition comprising 225 putts and then repeating the putting task again under low and high stress. Half the participants completed the training condition by putting in front of a video camera that was recording their performance, while half the golfers completed the training condition while having to do a secondary task (listening out for a particular word played on a tape). The researchers induced high stress by telling participants that if their putting performance improved by 20% they could win some money. The golfers who practiced putting in front of a video camera improved performance under pressure.

Application

Paying attention and consciously thinking about movements can lead to poor performance. Golfers placed under pressure can sometimes consciously focus on making sure stroke movement is done correctly in an effort to do well, but this makes the usually automatic movement less smooth (paralysis by analysis). Getting golfers used to performing under a condition that made them pay attention to their movements inoculated them against the likelihood of doing so while under pressure. It also shows the importance of 'training to compete' – replicating the stress of competition in practice such that the ability to cope with pressure can be developed.

Key Point

One way to control the tendency to pay attention and consciously control movements, when under pressure, is to practice under conditions similar to that of competition.

Beilock, S. L., & Carr, T. H. (2001). On the fragility of skilled performance: What governs choking under pressure? *Journal of Experimental Psychology-General,* 130, 701-725.

Research Bunker #18: Why does Tiger Woods wear red?

The Study

Tiger Woods is famous for wearing red on the final round of every major tournament. We do not know whether Tiger wears this out of habit, superstition or because he believes it gives him an advantage. But interestingly there is research evidence, albeit not from golf, that suggests that Tiger may gain an advantage from wearing red. In the 2004 Olympics, contestants who were assigned the red uniform or body protectors in boxing, Taekwondo, Greco-Roman wrestling and freestyle wrestling won more competitions than competitors assigned the blue uniform or body protector. This effect was particularly marked when the competitors were of similar ability. Determining why the colour red is associated with success is a little harder to unpick but it is thought that red may have evolutionary significance as a sign of dominance and threat.

Application

A golfer wearing red may feel more dominant and confident and the opponent less confident and a little intimidated, although it is difficult to imagine these are conscious feelings on behalf of the golfer.

Key Point

Wearing red seems to be associated with greater success in interactive sports where people compete directly against each other but whether this transfers to golf is yet to be determined.

Hill, R. A., & Barton, R. A. (2005). Red enhances human performance in contests. *Nature*, 435, 293.

Research Bunker #19: Take a conservative perspective on putting

The Study

Putting performance has been explored on the PGA tour. Rather than relying on the freely available data on putting performance such as the number of putts per round, or birdie conversion, a mathematical model was developed based on a data collection system known as ShotLink. This system captures the ball location and elevation for every putt to within 1 cm on the green. It provides a detailed analysis about putting performance because it gives a real indication of how difficult the putt was (e.g., distance, whether it is downhill putt, etc.).

Data were collected from 45 PGA tour events held at 30 courses from 2003 to 2008. An enormous number of data points were collected (more than 2 million) and interesting analyses were conducted including who was the best putter during that time (Tiger Woods) and whether putting performance is worse in the final pressure filled fourth round for players in contention (it is not).

One statistic, particularly, caught our eye and has implications for the psychological approach to putting. The likelihood of making a seven foot putt by a professional golfer is 50-50. That's right, the best professional putters will only make one out of every two putts from seven feet.

Application

Unrealistic expectations undermine the psychological approach to competition of many amateur golfers we meet. You will probably know of many amateur golfers who will berate themselves and 'beat themselves up' having missed a seven-foot putt and this rumination will go on to negatively affect their subsequent performance on the golf course. Yet, making a putt of that length is a 'coin toss' for even the best golfers.

By all means try to make putts of seven feet and more and make sure you are in the best shape to do so, for example through a well-worked pre-putt routine and a confident, relaxed stroke. But thinking you 'should' make these putts is not helpful and not true – even for professional golfers.

Key Point

When putting, be realistic about what can be achieved and keep focused on hitting a good putt, rather than focussing on what the outcome ought to be.

Fearing, D., Acimovic, J., & Graves, S. C. (2011). How to catch a Tiger: Understanding putting performance on the PGA TOUR. *Journal of Quantitative Analysis in Sports, 7,* Article 5.

Research Bunker #20: Varying practice helps your performance

The Study

Understanding the most effective way to practice golf skills is clearly important, particularly for those people who have just taken up the game. One phenomenon that can help inform practice is called 'contextual interference'. Put simply contextual interference is the interference in performance and learning which occurs when a task is practised in the context of other tasks. To explain, many people practice putting by doing the same putt from the same distance repeatedly. This is an example of practice with low contextual interference. Others may practice putting a few balls, then pitching, and then putting again. In the second example there is higher contextual interference because the putting is practised alongside a different skill – pitching.

In general, practice with low contextual interference enhances performance in practice settings but the transfer of learning to actual performance is lower, because the skill has been learnt in a very specific context and the transfer to performance where contexts continually vary is less.

To explore this, a study was conducted with 23 male novice golfers on putting and pitching. The putt was from 3.2 metres and the pitch was from 10.6 meters - both at an indoor target. After a baseline performance on both tasks the golfers were allocated to one of three groups. Seven golfers practised 80 putts followed by 80 pitches. Nine golfers did 10 putts followed by 10 pitches and repeated this sequence eight times. The final seven golfers alternated putting and pitching until all 160 shots had been done. When the participants completed a follow up test the best performing group in performance and movement technique (assessed by experienced golfers) was the group who alternated pitching and putting. The group with the highest contextual interference learned the skill best.

Application

So the next time you practise you may think about varying the shots you do, from club to club, or if you are using the same club, then vary the distances (e.g., follow up a 3 foot putt with a 10 foot putt). Variety is not only the spice of life but also the source of good practice!

Key Point

Varying your shots when practising will help performance in competition.

Porter, J. M., Landin, D., Hebert, E. P., Baum B. (2007). The effects of three levels of contextual interference on performance outcomes and movement patterns in golf skills. *International Journal of Sports Science and Coaching, 2,* 243-255.

Research Bunker #21: Social support matters on the course

The Study

The amount of social support received by amateur golfers was directly related to performance. Two days before a major competition, 117 high level amateur golfers completed a questionnaire which assessed the amount of social support they had received in the last week, along with the amount of stress they had experienced in relation to technical aspects, personal problems and competition pressure. Scores on the social support questionnaire were related to the golfers' actual performance in competition. The golfers who received greater social support performed better than those with lower social support. It was hypothesised that social support would benefit performance by buffering the potentially negative consequences of competition stress; however, social support did not appear to act in this way and rather seemed to be related to performance directly. Why social support relates to performance in this way is unclear but it is clear that receiving social support is beneficial for performance.

Application

If you are a coach, caddie, parent, or friend of a golfer, then one way in which you can help them perform in competition is to provide social support in the lead up to competition. Examples of the types of support that can be effective include tangible support, such as driving them to the driving range; informational support such as getting the correct yardage charts for the course; esteem support such as reminding the golfer of their talents; and emotional support such as listening to concerns about the upcoming competition.

Key Point

Providing support to a golfer can help them play better.

Rees, T., Hardy, L., Freeman, P. (2007). Stressors, social support, and effects upon performance in golf. *Journal of Sports Sciences, 25*, 33-42.

Research Bunker #22: Broken clubs and expletives – How do golfers cope with stress?

The Study

The headline from this insight is taken, in part, from the title of the paper which is summarised. It outlines why golfers experience stress and how they use a range of strategies to cope with stress. The research is based on interviews with 11 male golfers with a range of abilities, all of whom were studying at college in the United States. The golfers reported four major categories of stressors including evaluative others (e.g., people watching), specific performance challenges (e.g., challenging aspects of the course), psycho-emotional concerns (e.g., becoming frustrated) and competitive stress (e.g., the pressure of playing in a tournament). The six categories of techniques identified by the golfers on how they coped with stress included:

1. Cognitive techniques (e.g., using positive self-talk, imagining good shots)
2. Relaxation techniques (e.g., taking a deep breath)
3. Off-course efforts (e.g., reading articles in golf magazines or practising)
4. Golf-course strategies (e.g., playing smart, using clubs that you have confidence in)
5. Avoidance coping (e.g., talking to friends between shots to keep the mind off golf)
6. Emotion-focused coping (e.g., as the title indicates: breaking clubs, and cursing)

Application

The relevance of this research for the typical golfer is that it illustrates the variety of coping strategies that can be employed. Perhaps that is not surprising and we can all think of golfers who cope with stress differently and even employ a range of strategies to do so. The results also indicate how golfers can use practical techniques to cope with stress. For example, one of only two strategies (the other being avoidance-focused coping) that all eleven golfers said they used was golf-course strategies. This illustrates that one, very easy, and practical way to reduce stress is to think smart on the course. For example, when you find yourself under pressure, adopt a strategy for the upcoming hole that means you use the club with which you are most comfortable playing.

Key Point

Golfers use various coping strategies and simple, practical techniques, such as predominantly using the clubs you are most comfortable with, in order to effectively cope with stress.

Giacobbi, Jr. P., Foore, B. & Weinberg, R.S. (2004). Broken clubs and expletives: the sources of stress and coping responses of skilled and moderately skilled golfers. *Journal of Applied Sport Psychology, 16,* 166-182.

Research Bunker #23: Confidence buffers the effect of anxiety on performance

The Study

Data were collected from 7 amateur golfers during an 18-hole golf tournament, played according to Stapleford rules, to explore how anxiety and confidence interact to influence performance. Before each hole the golfers indicated on their scorecard how they felt on three psychological dimensions. These were cognitive anxiety (i.e. worry), somatic anxiety (i.e., the physical symptoms of anxiety such as a racing heart), and self-confidence. The performance of each golfer on the tee-shot for each hole was judged by two assessors who rated each shot based on the quality of the swing, distance the ball travelled, the trajectory of the ball in flight and the accuracy of the shot.

With these data it was possible for the authors to explore how performance was influenced by anxiety when the golfers reported experiencing high-levels of self-confidence and low-levels of self-confidence across the 18 holes. The results showed something quite interesting - that the interaction between cognitive anxiety and somatic anxiety on performance was different across high and low levels of confidence. To explain, when golfers lacked confidence, but had low levels of somatic anxiety, then increases in cognitive anxiety were associated with better performance. But when somatic anxiety was high then increases in cognitive anxiety were associated with a decrease in performance. So, when lacking in self-confidence, high levels of both cognitive and somatic symptoms of anxiety are bad for performance. In contrast, when the golfers were self-confident and had high levels of somatic anxiety then increases in cognitive anxiety did not have a negative influence on performance. This suggested that when confident, high levels of both cognitive and somatic aspects of anxiety need not have a negative effect on performance.

Application

This study illustrates how confidence is not only useful to acquire, in and of itself, but how it may help buffer the potential negative effects of anxiety on performance. Some of the common psychological skills that can be used to enhance confidence include positive self-talk and imagery.

Key Point

Feeling anxious is only a problem when a golfer does not feel confident. A golfer can build confidence by practising and improving as well as thinking positively about one's capabilities and imagining success.

Hardy, L., Woodman, T., & Carrington, S. (2004). Is self-confidence a bias factor in higher-order catastrophe models? An exploratory analysis. *Journal of Sport & Exercise Psychology, 26,* 359-368.

Research Bunker #24: Is there such a thing as a 'streaky' putter?

The Study

When it comes to putting, many golfers believe that they are either 'hot' or 'cold'. When they are 'hot', every putt seems to drop. But when they are 'cold', they couldn't buy a putt.

Some golfers believe there are 'streaky' putters and they will putt well for a while followed by a period when they putt poorly. But are people perhaps reading chance fluctuations as evidence of an elevated state of performance? Two researchers, David Gilden from the University of Texas and Stephanie Gray Wilson from Seton Hall University, examined this phenomenon amongst forty golfers in a laboratory setting. They reported that 'streaky' performance in golf did occur and was more likely to occur when the putts were not too difficult for the person. In short, it depends on the skill level of the player (i.e., how much they could control the outcomes). They reported unusual putting 'streaks' only for those with high hit rates in the putting task. It makes sense that the greater control one has over a task (e.g., while putting, no one can touch your ball), the more likely a streak will occur compared to a more chaotic sport like basketball where opponents can challenge the player for the ball.

Application

Our memory works neatly when we are putting well because it reminds us only of those putts that dropped in the hole while discounting those that didn't. But when we are putting poorly, our memory reminds us only of those putts that didn't drop into the hole. It makes sense to remind ourselves that we can putt well and that the next putt is likely to go into the hole

Key Point

Before you begin to putt, remind yourself of the putts that dropped into the hole.

Gilden, D.L., & Wilson, S.G. (1995). Streaks in skilled performance. *Psychonomic Bulletin and Review, 2*, 260-265.

Research Bunker #25: Which skills will earn you the most money in golf?

The Study

Common sense tells most golfers that if they want to shoot a low round consistently, then they should practise the short game. By extension, if you went to the golf practice range now, you should find most golfers chipping, putting or splashing shots from the bunker. But from our experience in golf, over many years, especially amongst amateurs, the most interesting aspect of golfers' practice is that they rarely see the chipping area, sand bunkers, or putting green as busy as the driving bays. So, what does the research say about the most important skills in golf?

According to current research, driving distance, putting proficiency, and accuracy of approach shots are statistically and economically important. Simply, professional golfers earn most money by demonstrating their ability in these skills. Sometimes driving accuracy and proficiency at recovering from sand bunker hazards emerge as important factors in this research. So should the driving bays be as busy as they are at the practice range? Yes, and no. Yes, the ranges are important for driving distance, the short game skills, especially putting are where time and effort really pays off.

Application

If you want to reduce your handicap quickly, put your putter in your hand more often than your irons. And when you put your irons in your hand, make sure they are wedges more often than long irons.

Key Point

Working the shorter clubs in your bag means your handicap will head in one direction: down

---

Shmanske, S., (2008). Skills, performance, and earnings in the tournament compensation model: Evidence from the PGA tour micro data. *Journal of Sport Economics, 6,* 644-662.

Research Bunker #26: How much time should you take over your putts?

The Study

Golf commentators and analysts blame the length of time a golfer takes over a putt when it does not drop in the hole. It seems that professional golfers can take too much time over a putt and as a result, putt poorly. But how long should a golfer spend over a putt? And does speeding up your putting routine and execution produce more holed putts?

Sian Beilock, from the University of Chicago, along with her colleagues examined these questions between novice and expert golfers. For the novice golfers, going slower improved performance whereas the skilled golfers performed better by going faster. Also, the skilled golfers performed better by taking less time to plan their putt.

Application

Putting better means paying attention to your skill level. If you are a low handicap golfer, spend less time preparing and executing your putt. If you are a high handicap golfer, take your time to prepare and execute your putt.

Key Point

Putting better is a matter of timing and when you are skilled at putting do not dwell on what you have to do.

Beilock, S.L., & Gonso, S. (2008). Putting in the mind versus putting on the green: expertise, performance time, and the linking of imagery and action. *The Quarterly Journal of Experimental Psychology, 1*, 1-13.

Research Bunker #27: Do good PGA professionals play better when Tiger Woods is around?

The Study

Is internal competition a good thing? One might suspect that promoting internal competition will mean greater success and improvement overall; however, recent research suggests that if there are large differences in skills and abilities, such differences might serve to reduce competitors' efforts.

Jennifer Brown, from the University of California at Berkeley, examined whether the presence of Tiger Woods (i.e., a superstar) affected the performance of other golfers in tournaments between 1999 and 2006. On average, higher-skill PGA golfers' tournament scores were 0.8 strokes higher (that is they performed worse) when Tiger Woods was in the field, compared to when he was not. Strangely, there was no effect for the lower-skill players' scores when Tiger was in the field.

Application

There are conflicting ways in which these data can be interpreted but our feeling is that when Tiger is playing those higher-skilled golfers, they felt they had to play really well to beat him – that they had to be close to perfect. This increase in expectation led to a decrease in performance. Tiger did not affect how they played but his mere presence did affect how they approached each round.

Key Point

Playing against superior opposition can hurt your performance in golf – if you think you must be perfect. Do not increase the pressure on yourself.

Brown, J. (2007). Quitters never win: The (adverse) incentive effects of competing with superstars. *Job Market Paper,* 1-35.

The Research Bunker #28: Do you overthink your putts? And is it helping your putting?

The Study

Have you ever holed a double-breaking putt or pitched out of the rough to two feet from the hole and been asked: "how did you do that?" It is often easier to play such a shot than trying to describe how you did what you did. Skills flow best without thinking about them.

Kristin Flegal and Michael Anderson wanted to know if describing how we execute a task can disrupt how the task is performed, later. They asked lower and higher skilled golfers to perform a novel putting task in which they had to sink three consecutive putts. Next, they either described what they remembered of the putting, or they performed an irrelevant verbal task. Then they putted again. Compared with the higher skilled golfers who completed the irrelevant verbal task, the higher skilled golfers who had described their putting were significantly impaired in their ability to sink three additional consecutive putts. There was no such effect for describing the putting task amongst the lower skilled golfers.

Application

Overthinking can affect our execution of skills like putting, especially if we are skilled at the task. Seeing and doing without excessive deliberate thinking about the task will serve more skilled golfers well.

Key Point

Golfers putt best when not paying much attention to aspects of the putting stroke. Well-learned skills just need a platform for execution.

Flegal, K.E., & Anderson, M.C. (2008). Overthinking skilled motor performance: Or why those who teach can't do. *Psychonomic Bulletin and Review, 5*, 927-932.

Research Bunker #29: Are professional golfers at the Masters getting better each year?

The Study

With improvements in technology, coaching, and practice, one might assume that performances are improving over time at major championships. But is this the case? Sangit Chatterjee and colleagues, at Northeastern University, decided to explore the nature and extent of improved performances among golfers in the Masters tournament since the 1930s. The results showed that there has been a staggering improvement over time, as well as increased competition, in this tournament. For instance, the mean score of the top 40 players between 1950 and 1959 was 295.9 and between 1990 and 1999, it had dropped to 287.4.

Application

The passing of time brings progress in many facets of the game. The cumulative effect of this progress is a lowering of scores and increased competition among the professionals at these competitions. So achieving success relative to others is harder, even if shooting lower scores is more common.

Key Point

With golf equipment manufacturing, coaching methods, and psychological preparation improving together, it is inevitable that scores at the Masters would fall over the passage of time.

Chatterjee, S., Wiseman, F., & Perez, R. (2002). Studying improved performance in golf. *Journal of Applied Statistics, 8,* 1219-1227.

Research Bunker #30: Should you play aggressively or conservatively for the best outcomes in golf?

The Study

Golf is an intriguing game because it lures the golfer into a sense of control and a positive expectation about the possible outcome of a golf shot. When forced to choose between a driver and a long iron, the driver always seems to win out. Dan Kirschenbaum and his colleagues explored positive illusions about shot outcomes amongst a sample of club golfers. In other words, the tendency for a golfer to anticipate the shot s/he plans will turn out better than it actually does. The research compared initial tee shots with club selections used when golfers were offered a second ball to hit. The second shots usually followed a more conservative plan. Importantly, these shots were much better than those when golfers used their initial plans.

Application

Golfers would fare much better on the golf course if they were conservative (dare we say realistic) in their club selection and planning for each shot. Recognising and counteracting this flaw within one's game could produce much better scores over a round of golf.

Key Point

Whatever your level, be aware of positive illusions and be realistic about what you can achieve. Golfers of varying skill levels can be affected by positive illusions into the possible outcome of golf shots.

Kirschenbaum, D.S., O'Connor, E.A., & Owens, D. (1999). Positive illusions in golf: Empirical and conceptual analyses. *Journal of Applied Sports Psychology, 1*, 1-27.

Summary

Golf is a psychologically challenging game for many reasons. First, golf is an untimed event so you must stay out on the course as long as it takes to complete the round. Second, you are generally 'alone' when you compete against an opponent (or the field) so must rely on yourself to play your best when it matters most. Some golfers do benefit from the presence of their caddie, of course. Third, on any given day, you might play the golf of your dreams (better than you have ever played before) yet not win the competition because someone else played better than you on that day. Fourth, there is lots of time between shots to think (or worry) about what has happened or what will happen in the game. Finally, not only do we play against others but we also typically watch their performances too. Sometimes, we will watch a player playing much better than us and sometimes we will watch a player playing much worse than us. Regardless of what is happening to them, we have to find a way of playing that focuses on *our game* only. For these reasons, the successful golfer is the one who copes best with these and other challenges in the game.

The successful golfer loves the challenges presented on and off the golf course. The successful golfer plans each practice session, prepares diligently for competition and plays the game with confidence and freedom. The successful golfer is optimistic and realistic. The successful golfer is continually striving to master himself or herself.

We part with a quote from Nick Faldo. It summarises much of why we love golf especially what it reveals about our character and what it takes to be successful.

 I left school and my parents supported me… I'd cycle to the course at Welwyn with this contraption on the front [of my bicycle] to hold my clubs, [I would] hit practice balls all morning, have a bit of lunch, then maybe chip and putt, then play 27 or 36 holes. Then I'd go home for my tea, then out to the garden shed where my parents put a light in so I could clean my clubs, and then I used to swing a pickaxe like a club to build up strength. Then I went to bed, slept, got up and did it all over again. And I loved it.

Nick Faldo

The Successful Golfer

Part 3

Being a confident performer

In this lesson we will outline what confidence is, why confidence is good for performance, and what factors affect confidence. Remember, you must understand confidence so you can improve it.

Confidence is the belief that you have in your ability to be successful – not to win each time you play, but to perform well regardless of how others play. Golfers have a level of confidence (by that we mean feeling confident or diffident) about their performance in general, as well as a level of confidence for each of the individual elements that contribute to performance in golf.

Sometimes the levels of confidence may be similar across each element. For example, a golfer may feel moderately confident in his ability to hit a chip-and-run shot under a blustery wind, moderately confident in his driving, and moderately confident in his downhill putting.

Confidence levels, however, can also vary substantially across the different skills a golfer has to perform – and perhaps this is more common. For instance, a golfer may have a very high level of confidence in her ability to hit a 3 iron but a very low level of confidence in her ability to escape effectively from bunkers.

So, confidence is multi-faceted because it relates not only to how we feel in general about golf but *also* how we feel about all the specific things we have to do when playing golf. The more confident we feel about the many skills we have to perform on the golf course, the better. This means we must feel confident about a whole range of technical, tactical, physical and psychological skills that we need when playing golf.

We would now like to outline why a high level of confidence is good for golf. First, confident golfers exert more effort, especially in the face of difficulties, than less confident golfers. Remember the old saying, "When the going gets tough - the tough get going." Even when things are not going their way, confident golfers believe things will get better. Imagine a golfer who has seen three birdie putts narrowly slide by the hole on the front nine and dropped a shot because her ball plugged in a bunker. Despite these setbacks she still keeps working hard – she does not dwell on errors - and she is only focused on hitting good shots on the back nine. Or a golfer who is 3 down with five holes to play in a matchplay event – but who is still working hard, being committed, is focused on every shot, and keeps looking for ways to put pressure on his opponent. These qualities are clearly evident in great golfers. In short, great golfers never seem to know when they are beaten by the course... or… by an opponent.

Second, confident golfers focus on what can be achieved, not on what might go wrong. Of course, being aware of what might go wrong is important, if for example, driving to the left on a particular fairway means that the shot to the green is harder it makes sense to avoid doing so. So, being aware of what might go wrong is important because it means steps can be taken to avoid hazards. But *dwelling* on what might go wrong and *allowing* these thoughts and feelings to become the focus of attention is not advantageous. Rather, a confident golfer is someone who focuses on what good things they can do during a round, and on each hole, and not on what mistakes they might make.

Finally, confident golfers are not as badly affected by nerves as those lacking confidence. This does not mean that confident golfers don't feel anxious. Even supremely confident golfers sometimes have doubts. For instance, eight-time Major winner, Tom Watson, said after winning the 1981 Masters: "I was so nervous today I was almost jumping out of my skin all day. Usually when I'm playing decent, I'm nervous." What matters is that confidence inoculates golfers against the negative effects of anxiety because it prevents any worry from being a distraction and it stops golfers consciously thinking about the physical movements they have to do. This last point in particular is crucial for golf.

It would be strange if golfers did not feel at least some nerves. Going into competition and being nervous during an important round of golf is natural and to be expected. When confident golfers are worried they 'use' the worry as an incentive to invest extra mental effort into what they are doing. This means they are focused on what they have to do rather than on what they want to avoid. Anxious golfers who do not have confidence allow their worry to distract them.

As touched on above, confident golfers are less likely to consciously think about the movements they have to do when playing golf. This is important because consciously thinking about movements can lead to poor performance. This 'paralysis by analysis' happens when golfers are placed under pressure and in an effort to do well they consciously focus on making sure the movement is done correctly (e.g., when a golfer concentrates hard on making sure her putting stroke is correct – when actually trying to stroke the putt).

Paradoxically, concentrating on controlling a motor movement (like a putting stroke) usually leads to a worse performance because the movement becomes less fluid. Indeed, many of the techniques outlined in this book are aimed at preventing conscious control of motor movements. In effect the goal is for the golfer to play each shot without thinking about it.

To work out ways in which to enhance confidence it is necessary to understand what factors influence confidence levels. If we understand what increases (and decreases) confidence, then we have a sound basis for strategies that will help us enhance our confidence when we play. There are four main factors that influence our confidence: our past performance(s), verbal persuasion, modelling and emotional arousal.

Past Performance(s)

By far the most important factor that influences confidence is our past performances. This is not surprising because we feel confident about things that we have done well in the past. Success breeds success because success increases confidence. For example, many golfers report having a favourite venue where they have had success and because confidence is associated with performing well, they often go on to perform well at the venue again. This further reinforces the 'link' between the venue and success – creating a self-fulfilling prophecy. Likewise, negative performances can have the opposite effect on confidence. This holds true not only for venues but also specific holes and clubs. If we have confidence in a specific club we feel good about using it and are more likely to hit a good shot with it – reinforcing the link even further.

Verbal Persuasion

Verbal persuasion is also an important source of confidence and it can come from two main sources. First, there are comments from sources external to us such as an opponent or a coach. To illustrate, a coach may seek to enhance a golfer's confidence by reminding her of the excellent training she has done in the last month, whereas an opponent may choose to remind the golfer of a poor performance the last time they met. Clearly, these two individuals are trying to have different effects on the golfer's confidence levels!

An often-overlooked source of verbal persuasion is what golfers say to themselves. It is common to see golfers across all levels berating themselves after an error. Often this can be a simple case of venting frustration, and is perfectly understandable - such as a golfer who has missed a birdie putt after an excellent approach shot. Sometimes, however, the types of things we say out loud and the things we say in our own mind can have a more lasting effect about how we feel about golf.

A golfer who thinks "I keep hooking – I am playing appallingly," and then "I am playing rubbish – it is just not my day," and keeps running these thoughts over in his mind, is likely to find confidence levels deteriorating (and along with it performance levels) throughout the round. Often, because golfers are highly motivated individuals with a strong desire to improve, self-criticism – to some degree – is to be expected; however, the challenge (which we address later) is to find the way of maintaining your motivation to improve and to avoid a destructive spiral of self-criticism during competition that can reduce your confidence.

Modelling

Modelling is the third source of confidence and comes from observing others doing the same task. For example, seeing a playing partner getting up and down from a difficult bunker may help a golfer feel able to do the same. For modelling to have an effect on confidence it is important that the model is perceived to be of similar status to the observer. Put simply, if a golfer observes someone who he perceives as much better than him executing a task, this will have no effect on the belief in his ability to do the same thing. Seeing Phil Mickelson hit a pitch to within four feet will do little for the average club golfer's confidence - "He is so good it is no surprise he was able to do that."

Emotional Arousal

The final source of confidence is emotional arousal. We take our cue from our body as to whether we are ready to compete and for all golfers it is important that we find the right level of emotional arousal. This can be very personal. For example, one golfer may be lacking confidence about an upcoming competition if he feels 'flat'. In contrast, another golfer may find himself lacking confidence if, before the game, he feels too emotionally aroused and the butterflies are churning in his stomach.

Should golfers feel confident about shooting a good score?

Before considering how to maintain and improve confidence, it is important to be clear what factors golfers should feel confident about.

Many golfers ask whether they should feel confident about shooting a good score and think that this is what their focus should be. This is understandable because golf is a competitive game.

Golfers should feel confident that they will perform well and before a round of golf they should focus on what they have to do to perform well – this is what's in the golfer's control. In many ways, golf is a competition against the course, so shooting a good score is certainly important.

Usually, if a golfer is sufficiently talented and well prepared, then if she performs well she will likely shoot a good score. It is impossible, however, to say that every time a golfer plays well they will shoot a good score because there is always the chance that, on any given day, the bounce of the ball will work against them or good putts may slide past the hole. Remember, we are aiming for consistency and the score will take care of itself.

Therefore, it is important to remember:

HIGH LEVEL OF CONFIDENCE	➔	GOOD PERFORMANCE	➔	Shoot a Good Score (on most occasions!)
HIGH LEVEL OF CONFIDENCE	➔	GOOD PERFORMANCE	➔	WIN (on most occasions!)

Golfers can shoot a good score and lose, or play badly and win; however, in general it is important that golfers remember:

> THE FIRST STEP TO SHOOTING A GOOD SCORE IS TO PLAY WELL AND CONFIDENT PLAYERS PLAY WELL
>
> THE FIRST STEP TO WINNING IS TO PLAY WELL AND CONFIDENT PLAYERS PLAY WELL
>
> SO…
>
> FOCUS ON BEING CONFIDENT ABOUT PLAYING WELL.

This focus on personal performance is illustrated neatly in the oft-quoted saying – "Control the controllables." Focus on playing well and hitting good shots.

Goal setting

Goal setting is a useful psychological technique because it allows you to quantify your motivation, build confidence in your game, and remain committed to your most cherished dreams.

Goals might include winning a Sunday medal or national championship (i.e., outcome goals). Goals might also include working on the movement of your club head away from your ball (i.e., process goals). Both goals serve a purpose because the former encourages us in the long-term and the latter keeps us focused on those elements that allow us to play shots well. We need both goals but we focus most on process goals.

Goals work best when they fulfil certain criteria. You might be familiar with the *SMART* principle. SMART represents Specific, Measurable, Action-oriented, Realistic, and Timetabled. Let's deal with each one in turn.

Specific – is your goal presented in clear behavioural terms? For example, rather than saying I'm off to the range to work on my short game, you could say I will work on my bunker play today trying to land three out of every 10 balls within three feet of the cup.

Measurable – is your goal giving you feedback about your progress toward this goal? Without some feedback, we will not know whether we are improving. We suggest you keep a diary of your shots. For instance, you might choose to hit five golf balls to five different targets with five different clubs. You can record whether the ball landed on your target or landed to the left or right. You might make a note of the distance from the target also. This information will help you to understand your level of accuracy with different clubs.

Action-oriented – are your goals related to concrete actions? We mention action and behavioural terms here because these elements motivate us to continue working and improving. A simple way to check whether your goals are action-oriented is to ask yourself: is there a specific action identified in what I am doing? For instance, a golfer might say I want to get better at putting; however, to make this a specific action, he would say that, "I'm going to spend 45 minutes stroking 50 putts from the centre of the practice green to the first cut of grass to improve my feel for lag putting."

Realistic – are your goals possible given your skills and ability at this time? You might wish to hit 60% of the fairways with your drives rather than expecting to hit all drives exactly down the fairway. After all, even the best golfers in the world do not always hit all the fairways all the time. You might expect to roll all your seven-foot putts into the hole but as you will have read in the Research Bunker earlier, even the best Tour professionals only manage to score 50% of these putts at any time.

Timetabled – do you have a timetable to achieve your goals? Goals that are not timetabled do not fill us with confidence and motivation because we do not know when we intend to achieve these goals. It's a sensible plan to schedule a realistic timetable for your goals. For instance, you might want to improve your lag putting this year but rather than this vague goal you might plan to improve your lag putting percentage by 30% within the next eight weeks.

In summary, goal setting works to help you achieve your goals as long as you work on your goal setting. It's a good plan to write your goals in a notebook and then keep the notebook in your bag for each practice session. Here is an example for you.

Goal Setting (Example)

A general goal might be: I want to improve my pitching. A SMART goal would be as follows:

Specific: I want to improve my pitching from 35 yards (currently, I hit 20% of my pitches within three metres of the flag).

Measurable: I will record the landing distances of 50 pitches from my target. These will be recorded whether they are long, short, left or right of the target.

Action-oriented: I will take 50 pitches from various lies in my practice session.

Realistic: I aim to get 50% of my pitches within three metres of the flag.

Time-tabled: I will achieve my goal in eight weeks by practising three evenings per week.

Say the Right Things - Self-talk

When we talk about our psychological approach to competition we often mean what we think. It is no surprise that what we think, and in effect 'say to ourselves', can influence how we perform. The types of thoughts in our mind when we play can be considered our own 'personal coach' that can help us play well or - all too often - can also make us play badly.

What we say to ourselves can serve many purposes. Our self-talk can be motivating ("keep going"), it can help to control anxiety ("relax"), it can be a boost ("you have been striking the ball well on the range"), or it can be a blow ("my opponent looks good").

It is too simplistic, and indeed wrong, to say that all negative self-talk (e.g., "my opponent looks good") is always going to make us play badly because self-talk of this nature can have positive effects on our performance, for example, increasing motivation. However, being aware of the types of things you say to yourself and their consequences is important. To help with this process you may want to write down examples of negative self-talk that you experience during competition and outline what examples of positive self- talk (thoughts) you could have to replace them.

Negative Self-Talk	Positive Self-Talk

Pay attention to what you say to yourself, and when you catch yourself talking negatively - replace the negative statement with a positive one.

In turn, you do not have to wait until you catch yourself saying something negative to say something positive. Positive self-talk can be applied at any time. Be pro-active in making sure your thoughts are positive and relevant to what you want to do.

In general, unless you are consciously using negative self-talk to motivate yourself when playing golf it makes sense to ensure that your self-talk is positive. Positive self-talk can maintain or increase confidence and confidence is associated with better performance and increased effort – exactly what is needed when playing! Think about the thoughts you have, and the things you say to yourself, as an opportunity to be your own coach. You have an opportunity to tell yourself exactly what you need to do well. In effect, you should:

"Be a Good Coach to Yourself."

Imagine what a good golf coach would say to you in any particular situation and then say that to yourself. Golfers often know what should be done, and what they would say, if they were coaching someone else. For example, after an error, a golfer expects the coach to say, "head up, keep going, stay focused," whereas golfers will often say to themselves "you stupid idiot!" (Or words that are occasionally stronger). In short we may behave differently towards others than to ourselves.

So, in short, when playing golf, focus on what you need to do to succeed; typically this involves task relevant thoughts (e.g., strategy, maintaining motivation) and being positive. Just say to yourself exactly what the *best coach in the world* would say to you and "Be a Good Coach to Yourself."

To think positively, as a good coach would, is a challenge because, when we are placed under pressure, we often think the worst. If thinking positively was not a challenge, then everyone would do it and there would be no need for you to consider how this could be developed. However, you can train your mind to think more positively.

The mind has a limited capacity to process information (some more than others!) but this means that if you can fill your mind up with thoughts that will help you do well then there is less (or indeed no) room for any negative thoughts. The more your mind is filled up thoughts you need to succeed, the less space there is for negativity.

The great thing about our minds is that we can consciously choose what we want to think – for example, on the first tee of an important competition to prevent negative thoughts coming in, a golfer might say, "I have been striking the ball well in practice – let's show them what I can do when I pay attention to a good pre-shot routine." You can also use cue cards to remind yourself what to think and say to yourself. Write out on a cue card the types of positive things that will help you play well. You can laminate this card and put it in your golf bag and read this before and during your round of golf. These key words can be positive or instructional such as "smooth takeaway" or "eyes on the back of the ball".

Imagining the Right Things - Imagery

The strongest predictor of confidence is to 'know' we have mastered our skills. So, it can be difficult to feel confident about something until you have actually done it! This fact does present golfers (and psychologists) with a dilemma. How is it possible to feel confident about something you have not yet achieved? For example, how could a golfer who has never won a tournament feel confident about winning one? Well one especially effective way is to imagine success.

Imagery is an excellent strategy to help golfers prepare for competition, and simply it means running an action (e.g., pitch shot) or an event (e.g., winning a competition) over in your mind, seeing it as clearly and vividly as possible.

Imagery can be done from within your body (as you normally see the world) or from outside your body (as if you were watching yourself on TV). The style you choose depends on your personal preference; however, imagery is not only about seeing events in your mind's eye, it involves all of the senses to make re-creating the event as real as possible. To illustrate, a golfer imagining a successful pitch would feel the correct movements, feel and hear the ball come off the club face, see the ball travel through the air, see it pitch on the green, and hear it hit the flag and drop into the hole.

Ideally, as many of the senses should be used to make the imagery as realistic as possible but this will depend on your preference. Some people find it difficult to 'see' what is happening but are able to recreate the movement easily and vice versa. For example, Tiger Woods prefers to feel, rather than see, his golf shots.

Whatever your preference, or your ability, you can use imagery to build your confidence and enhance your golf game. Imagery is effective because the sensations imagined are 'real' to the mind. You may be able to recall how vivid dreams seem (particularly those we had as children) even though the events did not actually happen. Imagery is the same.

When we imagine, it activates the same areas of the brain that would normally be activated when the event is happening for real. With practice, imagery can be improved and made more realistic. The potential that can be achieved is again illustrated by recalling how realistic dreams can seem. So to enhance confidence you can:

- Recall times when you have done well. Replay success over and over in your mind in as much detail as possible. Use all the senses, in particular, the feelings associated with success. This is like carrying around your own personal 'greatest hits' tape in your head.
- Imagine success in an upcoming event. Picture yourself playing well and achieving success in as much detail as possible. Use all the senses, in particular, the feelings associated with success.
- Use imagery before specific golf skills. See the correct outcome, feel the correct movement pattern and then 'do it'. You can easily see how this could be applied to a number of skills (e.g., before every putt, before every drive, and so on).

165

The Successful Golfer

When using imagery there are three crucial points to remember. First, it is important to make sure the image occurs in 'real time' - the same speed it happens in real life. Second, always make sure that the imagery is positive – something you want to happen and not something you wish to avoid. Finally, it is vitally important that you practice imagery. Like all skills (mental and physical) the more you practice imagery the better you get. Our advice is to practice a little, often. Maybe spend 4 to 5 minutes a day imagining the shots you want to hit. Become comfortable using imagery in a low stress situation, first. For example, in a quiet comfortable room at home. When you find you are able to use imagery comfortably in that context then you can consider transferring it to situations where you may want to use it but where it's a bit more difficult to imagine - for example the driving range, the changing room or the clubhouse.

Many golfers use imagery as part of a pre-shot routine – that is a sequence of behaviours before striking the ball. In this situation, where the imagery has to be used on the golf course, we would recommend becoming comfortable imagining all the shots you can play at home; by all means imagine while holding the golf club – this has been suggested to make the image more realistic. Then integrate the imagery into part of your pre-shot routine on the driving range, become comfortable using it there before it is incorporated into your pre-shot routine out on the course.

We hope you can see the sequential way in which the skill is learned and practised - first in a low stress situation (at home) before being transferred to a moderate stress situation (the driving range) and then finally transferred to the high stress situations where it is needed (out on the golf course).

Practise and rehearse imagery even when the skill is learned. Remember if you want to use imagery before every drive then make sure you use it before every drive in practice. Jack Nicklaus said he never hit a drive, in either practice or competitions, without seeing where he wanted the ball to go. If you want to use imagery before every round then use it before every session at the driving range. Make it an integral part of your practice and competition. You choose when you want to use this effective and flexible skill – the night before a round, the morning of a round, as you are waiting to compete, or before executing each shot. Decide when it is right for you. If you are using imagery to build confidence then the imagery is about success – whether it is executing a particular shot, winning a competition, or playing well.

Breathing Exercises

Many golfers we work with tell us that they are unaware of their breathing on the golf course or while they practise. Some golfers, however, admit that they struggle to inhale deeply when they try it on the golf course during competition. For these golfers, we identified a need to integrate relaxation techniques into their mental skills training programmes using a three-stage approach.

In stage one, we used Progressive Muscular Relaxation (PMR) to help the golfers recognise and feel the difference between muscular tension and muscular relaxation. In stage two, we adopted a 'centring' technique to help the golfers control their breathing. This centring technique was integrated into the warm-up routine to become an integral and habitual element for competition. The golfers practised these techniques until they had gained competency in each, and felt comfortable doing these skills. In the final stage, we worked with the golfers to build these skills into training and competition routines. At this stage, the golfers were able to assess their own tension and apply the skills they learned to reduce unwanted tension.

Here is a brief description of centring that could be used to cope with mild anxiety and tension on the golf course. Remember to practise this technique as much as possible at home, or in practice sessions, before taking it to the golf course. You should feel comfortable using this technique in practice before using it in competition.

First, relax your neck and shoulder muscles by gently rolling your head and shoulders. Second, breathe deeply into your stomach instead of high up in your chest. When you breathe deeply into your stomach, you will notice your stomach bulging when you inhale and collapsing when you exhale. We suggest golfers breathe in for four seconds, and breathe out for eight seconds. On exhaling, the golfer can whisper a calming word: r-e-l-a-x or s-m-o-o-t-h. Centring is a useful technique in golf because the pre-shot routine gives us time to concentrate on our breathing. And because centring takes our focus to complete correctly, it directs our attention away from those thoughts that might be worrying us.

Pre-shot Routine

The pre-shot routine is a physical and mental sequence of actions to help golfers remain focused on the task at hand to play shots consistently well. Though the best golfers in the world might differ in the style of their swing, you will notice a similar sequence of actions for every shot. For instance, they will have a certain number of practice swings before setting up to the ball followed by a specific number of glances toward the target.

As well as a pre-shot routine, most golfers will also have a post-shot or post-mistake routine to allow them to recognise what went wrong with their swing or putt, and engage in a preferred action sequence. For example, after a poor swing, you will notice some golfers repeat their preferred swing. In match play, some golfers retake the missed putt before heading to the next tee.

Why are routines important? Routines are important for at least three reasons. First, they allow the golfer to remain consistent in the fundamentals of the set-up. The golfer can ensure that her grip, alignment, stance and posture are consistent each time she prepares for a shot. The best golfers in the world are always working on these fundamentals. Second, rather than thinking about irrelevant aspects of the game, such as the score or your opponent's shot to the green, you can pay attention to what you need to do to play your shot well. Finally, routines that are well practised help us to move from conscious attention to unconscious attention - to execute the shot at hand. In other words, once we have engaged in a physical and mental sequence that is well learned, we can allow the shot to unfold without consciously attending to the mechanics of the swing. We let the swing do its thing.

A useful way to develop a pre-shot routine is to consider the acronym PAR. This acronym can represent: *Preparation*, *Action*, and *Revision*.

In the *Preparation* section, you can assess the shot at hand. For example, you might examine the lie of your ball, the wind speed and direction, the pin placement and any particular hazards you need to avoid. Then you plan the shot that is best for you, considering your skills and ability at this time. The advice we offer here is be conservative but confident. In other words, choose conservatively but play confidently.

Once you have decided on the shot you intend to play, and the club you intend to use, you can swing the club or putter to feel the shot you wish to make while imagining the flight or path of the ball. Create a clear picture of what you want to happen. Now, you can step into the ball and ensure your grip, alignment, stance and posture is right for your shot.

In the *Action* stage, you will have set-up correctly to the ball and you are about to begin your swing sequence. Some golfers engage in an action to begin their swing such as a forward press of the club while other golfers sit back into their posture. Others just begin to take away their club when they feel ready. One useful sequence of actions we have found beneficial for allowing the swing to begin, without conscious control, has been the following: Target – Ball – Smooth Away. The golfer looks at the Target for the final time, then draws his eyes back to the Ball and Smoothly draws his club away from the ball. This sequence is beneficial for two reasons. First, the golfer can pay attention to the two things that matter most at this stage: his target and letting his swing do its thing. Second, it reduces the 'thinking time' for golfers who might begin to worry about unnecessary things to play their best golf.

The final stage, *Revision*, is a vital element of the pre-shot/post-shot routine because it allows the golfer to accept the outcome of the shot and move on to the next one. Most golfers will think and feel a particular way after they have hit their shots because they will have spent a lifetime watching the outcome of each shot they have ever hit. Good shots give us good feelings and we begin to think good things about ourselves. When other golfers see our good shots they usually say "well done, great shot," which acknowledges your competence in golf. After a poor shot, however, they might remain silent or say something like: "don't' worry about that one, you can get up and down from there." If we allow them, poor shots will prompt us to think and feel negatively about our golf game and ourselves. Golfers with a sound self-image know that one or a few poor shots are normal in golf and they can recover from them. They know that poor shots do not make them 'bad golfers' or 'bad people'. They keep the entire game in perspective.

It is a sensible idea to learn to accept the outcome of each shot as an objective measure of where the ball travelled. What we mean here is *not* to attach any valuations about *you* to the outcome of the shot. This is a challenging but worthwhile thinking skill to learn. If the ball consistently travels further left than you would wish, you can ask your teaching professional to examine your swing when you leave the golf course.

Perfect Practice Makes Perfect

The following guidelines are offered to build effective practice sessions:

1. Plan your session before you go to the practice range.

You should set a rule for yourself never to go to the practice range without a written plan for what you intend to do. Remember to follow the SMART principle outlined above to build goals for your practice session.

2. Organise a suitable time to start and finish your session.

Each practice session should have a defined start and finish time. This organisation helps you to keep your sessions short and sharp rather than long and ill-defined. Short sharp sessions keep your mind focused on what you want to achieve.

3. Warm-up and stretch before you begin your practice.

Golf is a physical game requiring distinct ranges of motion, for instance, in your shoulders, arms, and hips. Golf also requires dynamic movement to propel the golf ball off the tee and out of thick rough. Because golf requires these ranges of motion and dynamic movement, the execution of shots depends upon the coordinated movement of various body parts. If you have not stretched your hips and shoulders, it's likely that you will not make a full shoulder turn when required to hit the ball precisely. It's sensible to warm-up and stretch before you begin.

4. Begin by practising your best skills, first.

You can gently ease your way into the practice session by practising your best skills, first. Not only are you gently preparing your body for the physical demands later but also you are building confidence by reminding yourself how well you swing your clubs.

5. Build your pre-shot routine into every shot you practice.

Practice is the one place where you can organise yourself to prepare and play golf well. You are master of your destiny on the practice ground. Make sure you integrate your pre-shot routine into every shot you practice so that practice is organised, purposeful and focused. If sloppiness and laziness creep into your practice sessions, they will also creep into your game on the golf course.

6. Ensure that each shot you take is focused on a target.

Golf is a target-oriented sport. When golfers play on the golf course, they usually aim their bodies and clubs toward a target. With this fact in mind, we should ensure that every shot we take on the practice range also has a target. For example, if you are pitching a ball out of thick rough, you might aim it toward a particular target on the green allowing the ball to roll out to the hole.

7. Simulate conditions you will encounter on the course.

The conditions you practice under on the range should be similar to the conditions you will be playing on the golf course. It is not always possible to simulate the emotional rollercoaster that is presented in competitive golf but we can aim to create conditions as close as possible to it.

It is not always possible to find uphill and downhill lies that match the conditions on a particular course, but our aim is to find conditions as close as possible to these. If you practise without considering the various thoughts and feelings as well as the environmental conditions you will encounter on the golf course, then you are failing to prepare properly for the examination on the course.

8. Integrate massed and distributed practice into your session.

Practising your skills properly requires a focus on your needs right now. Massed practice is appropriate to learn specific skills or make specific changes to your swing. You might require consistent practice of a particular element of the swing to 'groove' that movement. Distributed practice means practising for shorter periods over a longer timeframe. For instance, you might spend time practising various chip shots and pitches in short periods and practise them over the longer term. Your specific needs, outlined by your teaching professional, will guide you toward massed and distributed practice sessions.

9. Record your performance and set skills tests for yourself.

It's difficult to know whether you are improving or not if you do not have some record of your performance. You might consider yourself a good bunker player yet a skills test might persuade you otherwise. What you thought you could achieve and what you actually do achieve show a mismatch. This skills test would be a useful way to assess your current form. In some instances, however, a golfer may not perform well in a skills test (because he or she is not motivated by the test) yet perform competently in a competitive game.

10. Reward yourself consistently during your practice session.

Many of the golfers we support in our consultancy do not reward themselves for their effort and achievement during practice sessions. In golf practice, for example, you might reward yourself with encouraging statements (e.g., well done, maintain your relaxed focus), a new piece of equipment or even a day off from practice. These rewards depend on you setting and achieving a specific goal. Rewards reinforce our good behaviour.

Practising for the Real Thing

We have recommended that you practise golf as you intend to play on the course. So you might practise hitting shots from thick rough or with an awkward stance in the bunker; however, these environmental simulations often lack those specific thoughts and feelings that are typical during the final holes of an important competition. It is important to think about how you will cope with the various challenges you encounter on the course. These challenges can be a mix of environmental modifications (e.g., playing with wet gloves) and psychological demands (e.g., playing in front of a vocal audience). We have presented some examples below that you can integrate into your golf practice.

Get your heart racing

Putting on the practice green rarely resembles the conditions you experience when you are trying to putt a seven-footer for par to make the cut on the 18th green. It's likely that your heart rate and blood pressure will be raised as you confront this challenge. You can prepare physiologically for this situation by doing some physical exercise such as 10 press-ups or a 20-metre sprint. Then return to your ball, compose yourself and go through your pre-shot routine. Your elevated heart rate will resemble what you might experience physiologically on the 18th green.

Set a public challenge

You can set-up a public challenge to hole 25 four-foot putts in a row or land 10 bunker shots within 6 feet of a pin. You might even set the challenge against another player in a putt-off. The first player to miss a putt loses the putt-off. The audience can support or distract you to resemble conditions in a tournament. These public challenges are a useful way to practise for the 'heat of battle' you might encounter during a competitive tournament.

Enjoy the rain

Many golfers are disappointed when the rain falls before they play a round of golf. And many of the golfers we support tell us that they avoid practising in the rain and hence are less prepared for the challenges the rain brings. It is not always possible to train in the rain; however, it is possible to soak your grips and your gloves (and your clothes if you wish) to create the challenging circumstances you will face on the course.

Get the cameras rolling

If you do not have an audience but you do have a video camera, you can set up the camera to record your practice as if you were on television. You need to prepare diligently for each shot as if you were on television and the best golf coaches were going to analyse your shots. If you do not have a video camera, you can ask yourself: How would I behave if there was a camera recording everything I do in practice? Then practise as if the camera was recording you - from the beginning to the end of your practice session.

Reflect on the Right Things

As discussed, our confidence can be affected by what happens when we play golf. It is important, therefore, that we give some thought to how we reflect on golf competition in a way that helps us develop and progress in the best way possible. In short, after each round, golfers should maintain a balanced perspective on what they have achieved and how they can improve.

The general tendency, following success, is to accept it without question and to attribute it to internal causes - "I shot a good score because I am a good ball striker." The tendency, following a poor performance or a defeat, is to search for a reason why - "I lost because I lacked the fitness in the last few holes." Therefore, the tendency following success is to engage in thought processes that boost confidence further (at the *expense* of identifying areas to improve) while following defeat or a poor performance, the tendency is to engage in thought processes that reduce confidence (whilst *overemphasising* areas that need improving). This is a simple distinction but it does describe what usually occurs.

Of course, searching for reasons why you performed poorly does make sense because if you can address those reasons then you will improve – but this should not be done at the expense of your confidence levels. Golfers should also focus on, and remind themselves about, what went well during a game. Every round of golf, regardless of whether you have won, or lost, performed well or performed poorly, is a chance to improve and get better. Logically the thought processes should be the same after every round – but left to our own devices, and natural thought processes, this is not the case.

To encourage golfers to reflect in a balanced manner on each performance, and to use each performance as a springboard to improvement while crucially maintaining confidence, we ask golfers to reflect on past performances in the following manner: by writing down three things that went well during the performance and one aspect that they can improve on. It is also important to indicate how this aspect *can* be improved (e.g. 30 minutes extra putting training from 6-10 feet) – after all indicating *what* needs improving without indicating *how* this will be done does not mean much.

In addition, reflecting on competition in this manner also allows a golfer to build up a record of all the good things they have achieved. The three good things achieved per round can be transferred to an achievement log which is simply a list of each round of golf and the three good things the golfer did. In short, it is possible to develop a substantial record of achievement that can be revisited to boost confidence whenever it is needed (e.g., before an important competition).

Further Information

The information we have provided in this section, and throughout this book, represents some of the practical support you would receive when you consult a chartered sport psychologist. The support you would receive from a chartered sport psychologist in face-to-face sessions (or through Skype/telephone) is tailored to meet your specific needs, which you might consider is most appropriate for you. If you would like more information, or if you would like to meet for further support, you can contact Marc or myself through: www.drpaulmccarthy.co.uk

References

Page 3: Frank Keating, The Guardian, September 23, 1989.

Page 4: Nicky Campbell, Guardian Sport, September 28, 2006.

Page 5: Harry Talbot, The Sun, October 13, 2005

Page 5: Art Spander, The Daily Telegraph, September 28, 2006

Page 13: Alexzndra Oyston, The Daily Telegraph, February 17, 2005

Page 15: Sunday Life, October 9, 2011

Page 17: Brian Keogh, The Sunday Times, August 17, 2008.

Page 19: Jack Nicklaus, The Daily Telegraph, July 18, 2006.

Page 21: Mark Fleming, The Express, August, 11, 2004

Page 23: Nick Pitt, The Sunday Times, June 14, 2009.

Page 25: Andy Farrell, The Independent, April 1, 2003.

Page 27: Derek Lawrenson, The Observer, July 16, 1995.

Page 29: Peter Dixon, The Times, September 9, 2006.

Page 31: James Lawton, The Independent, June 18, 2013.

Page 33: Paul Mahoney, The Independent, April 11, 2013

Page 35: Jim White, The Guardian, July 15, 2002

Page 37: Simon Jones, The Independent, December 11, 1995

Page 39: Denis Walsh, The Sunday Times, December 16, 2007

Page 41: Bill Elliott, The Observer, July 12, 2009

Page 43: Paul Kimmage, The Sunday Times, March 26, 2006

Page 45: John Hopkins, The Times, April 8, 2008

Page 47: Lewine Mair, The Daily Telegraph, February 26, 2008

Page 49: Alistair Tait, The Observer, July 14, 2002

Page 51: David Owen, The Observer, October 29, 2006

Page 53: Larry Dorman, The New York Times, August 9, 2011

Page 55: John Hopkins, The Times, January 19, 2009

Page 57: Darren Clarke and Karl Morris, Golf – The mind factor, p. 63, 2005

Page 59: Mike Selvey, The Guardian, July 22, 2002

Page 61: Lewine Mair, The Daily Telegraph, April 6, 2006

Page 63: Andy Farrell, The Independent, April 5, 2000

Page 65: Lewine Mair, The Daily Telegraph, October 26, 2005

Page 67: John Daly, My life in and out of the rough, Harper Sport, 2007

Page 69: Lewine Mair, The Daily Telegraph, September 30, 2006

Page 71: Lewine Mair, The Daily Telegraph, April 6, 2006

Page 73: Brian Keogh, The Sunday Times, June 19, 2011

Page 75: Lewine Mair, The Daily Telegraph, April 6, 2006

Page 77: One fine day, Sunday Tribune, November 5, 2006

Page 79: Blaine Minn, Associated Press, August 7, 2011

Page 81: John Hopkins, The Times, April 8, 2008

Page 83: Denis Walsh, The Sunday Times, July 29, 2007

Page 85: Matt Dickinson, The Times, May 14, 2011

Page 87: Denis Walsh, The Sunday Times, December 16, 2007

Page 89: Andy Farrell, The Independent, August 1, 1999

Page 91: Brian Alexander, The Guardian, May 19, 2000

Page 93: John Hopkins, The Times, January 22, 2007

Page 95: James Corrigan, The Sunday Telegraph, March 24, 2013

Page 97: Jack Nicklaus, The Daily Telegraph, July 18, 2006

Page 99: Matthew Syed, The Times, July 16, 2008

Page 101: Rick Broadbent, The Times, May 11, 2011

Page 103: Peter Dixon, The Times, May 17, 2011

Page 105: Paul Kelso, The Daily Telegraph, July 18, 2011

Page 107: John Hopkins, The Times, February 12, 2001

Page 109: Peter Dixon, The Times, July 19, 2012

The Successful Golfer

Page 111: Weekend Sport, The Independent, July 18, 1992

Page 113: Jack Nicklaus, The Daily Telegraph, July 18, 2006

Page 151: Alastair Campbell, The Times, March 13, 2004

Graduation: Life Lessons of a Professional Footballer by Richard Lee

The 2010/11 season will go down as a memorable one for Goalkeeper Richard Lee. Cup wins, penalty saves, hypnotherapy and injury would follow, but these things only tell a small part of the tale. Filled with anecdotes, insights, humour and honesty - Graduation uncovers Richard's campaign to take back the number one spot, save a lot of penalties, and overcome new challenges. What we see is a transformation - beautifully encapsulated in this extraordinary season.

"Whatever level you have played the beautiful game and whether a goalkeeper or outfield player, you will connect with this book. Richard's honesty exposes the fragility in us all, he gives an honest insight into dimensions of a footballer's life that are often kept a secret and in doing so offers worthy advice on how to overcome any hurdle. A great read." **Ben Foster, Goalkeeper, West Bromwich Albion and England.**

Soccer Tough by Dan Abrahams

"Take a minute to slip into the mind of one of the world's greatest soccer players and imagine a stadium around you. Picture a performance under the lights and mentally play the perfect game."

Technique, speed and tactical execution are crucial components of winning soccer, but it is mental toughness that marks out the very best players – the ability to play when pressure is highest, the opposition is strongest, and fear is greatest. Top players and coaches understand the importance of sport psychology in soccer but how do you actually train your mind to become the best player you can be?

Soccer Tough demystifies this crucial side of the game and offers practical techniques that will enable soccer players of all abilities to actively develop focus, energy, and confidence. Soccer Tough will help banish the fear, mistakes, and mental limits that holds players back.

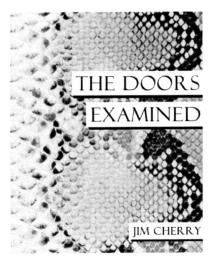

The Doors Examined
by Jim Cherry

Jim Morrison, Ray Manzarek, Robby Krieger and John Densmore. Welcome to the known, the unknown, and the in between.

The Doors remain one of the most influential and exciting bands in rock 'n' roll history, and The Doors Examined offers a unique, expressive insight into the history of the band, their influence on culture, and the group's journey following the death of Jim Morrison in Paris in 1971. It starts at the beginning, on a Venice Beach rooftop, and takes the reader on an invigorating journey, from The Whisky a Go-Go to the Dinner Key Auditorium, The Ed Sullivan Show to Père Lachaise Cemetery. Comprised of selected acclaimed articles from The Doors Examiner, The Doors Examined also serves up original content that assesses seminal albums, how the group's music has influenced other artists, and key people in the band's history; people like Jac Holzman, Paul Rothchild, Bruce Botnick, and Pam Courson.

Small Time: A Life in the Football Wilderness by Justin Bryant

In 1988, 23-year-old American goalkeeper Justin Bryant thought a glorious career in professional football awaited him. He had just saved two penalties for his American club - the Orlando Lions - against Scotland's Dunfermline Athletic, to help claim the first piece of silverware in their history. He was young, strong, healthy, and confident.

Small Time is the story of a life spent mostly in the backwaters of the game. As Justin negotiated the Non-League pitches of the Vauxhall-Opel League, and the many failed professional leagues of the U.S. in the 1980s and 90s - Football, he learned, is 95% blood, sweat, and tears; but if you love it enough, the other 5% makes up for it.

Around the World in 80 Scams: an Essential Travel Guide by Peter John

Every year, thousands of people fall victim to various travel scams, crimes and confidence tricks while they travel. Most people escape having simply lost a little money, but many lose much more, and some encounter real personal danger

This essential book is a practical, focused, and detailed guide to eighty of the most common scams and crimes travellers might encounter. It is packed with real-world examples drawn from resources across the globe and the author's own travels. Being aware of scammers' tricks is the best way of avoiding them altogether.

Chapters cover all sorts of scams including: Hotels and other accommodation scams, Transport scams, Eating, drinking and gambling scams, Begging and street hustling scams, extortion, blackmail and fraud scams, and more.

Saturday Afternoon Fever: A Year On The Road For Soccer Saturday
by Johnny Phillips

You might already know Johnny Phillips. He is a football reporter for Sky Sports' Soccer Saturday programme and a man who gets beamed into the homes of fans across the country every weekend.

For the 2012/13 season, Johnny decided to do something different. He wanted to look beneath the veneer of household-name superstars and back-page glamour to chronicle a different side to our national sport. As Johnny travelled the country, he found a game that he loved even more, where the unheralded stars were not only driven by a desire to succeed but also told stories of bravery and overcoming adversity, often to be plucked from obscurity into the spotlight… and sometimes dropped back into obscurity again. Football stories that rarely see the limelight but have a value all fans can readily identify with.

Lightning Source UK Ltd.
Milton Keynes UK
UKOW02f0418140813

215293UK00002B/64/P